Latin Crossword Puzzles

Usus magister est optimus
(Practice makes perfect)

Book 2

Michael Stachiw, Jr.

Latin Crossword Puzzles – Book 2
Copyright 2014
Printed in the United States of America
Published by SM&DS through Createspace Independent Publishing Platform
ISBN-13: 978-1503302303
ISBN-10: 150330230X

Latin - 1

Across

2. weakening; refusing; invalidating.
5. wish, will, inclination.
6. to cut off, to separate, take away.
8. purple, red.
11. quick, swift, rapid, speedy, fast.
13. delightful, pleasurable.
15. fortification, protection, defenses.
18. on account of, for the sake of.
19. openly, frankly.
20. related by blood, kinsman.
21. to consider carefully, weigh, ponder.
22. over, above; concerning, about, besides.

Down

1. beginning.
3. four times; again and again.
4. ensnare, trap, beguile, deceive, cheat.
7. to taste.
9. to flow, pour, stream.
10. hare, rabbit.
12. completely, wholly, fully.
14. to suspend, hang.
16. vain, useless, ineffectual, of not effect.
17. fear, dread, anxiety.

Latin - 2

Across

6. to injure, weaken, discourage, damage, break.
8. to turn away, avert, avoid. turn back.
11. to tinge, dye, stain, imbue.
13. to show oneself, present oneself.
14. to produce, engender.
16. composition, agreement, pact; arrangement.
18. eagerness, zeal.
19. death, ruin, annihilation.
21. at least, at all events.
22. loveliness, charm, attractiveness, beauty.
23. to graze, forage, browse.

Down

1. to punish.
2. master, canon; master of a school, professor.
3. admonition, warning.
4. able, mighty, powerful, strong.
5. to examine, treat of, discuss.
7. citizen, townsman, bourgeois, burgess.
9. triers.
10. to be silent, leave unmentioned.
12. false conclusions, logical fallacies.
13. at first, for the first time, in the first place.
15. violent, furious, impetuous.
17. dark-colored, blackish
20. foreign, acquired.

Latin - 3

Across

4. salty, witty.
6. feather; featherbed; pen.
14. skillfully.
16. old.
18. to compare, contrast; compete.
19. after, behind.
20. first, foremost; most distinguished, first.
22. morning, early in the morning, early.
23. tin.

Down

1. differently from, otherwise than.
2. subject, topic, theme.
3. shoot up, sprout, burgeon.
5. eternal, everlasting, without end.
7. to mix, mingle, blend.
8. pertaining to a bedroom
9. dog.
10. to forsake, desert, abandon.
11. chosen, select.
12. to fill, satisfy.
13. to stand, stand still, stand firm.
15. bookcase, case for papers.
17. to watch over, keep, protect, observe, save, reserve.
21. rule; monastic rule.

Latin - 4

Across

5. complaining, plaintive, whining.
6. to work, labor, toil, take pains.
10. to weep for, bewail.
12. in order to, for the sake of, to.
14. to grow accustomed to, used to, make familiar.
16. hindrance, impediment, obstacle, difficulty.
18. publication, promulgation.
19. pepper.
20. lamp.
21. far and wide.
22. newly, recently, not long ago.
23. thievish.
24. wonderful, astonishing, extraordinary.

Down

1. melior : optime : well, better, best
2. youth
3. before.
4. to establish, found, institute.
7. duty, service, job.
8. building, structure.
9. to deny, refuse, reject.
11. lentil.
13. to have a bad odor, stink.
15. a little knife.
17. a reader.
18. peace

Latin - 5

Across

2. beautify, embellish, adorn.
6. cover with earth, bury,
7. to enlarge, lengthen, extend; put off, defer.
10. a cake.
11. settled, resolved, decided.
13. to wish a person joy, congratulate ,give thanks
16. alleviation, improvement, mitigation.
18. to restore, repair; unite, reconcile.
21. fall, fault, error, sliding, graduate movement.
23. to die, wither away, decay.
24. to exempt from blame, excuse, make excuses, plead.

Down

1. manage, administer; provide money.
3. to compare.
4. pruner.
5. dusk, twilight.
8. to frighten, terrify, scare away, deter.
9. tested, tried, approved, experienced.
12. expense, cost.
14. even if, although.
15. to go back, come back, return; to come in.
16. to bind, tie.
17. loosening; payment.
19. secretly.
20. too much, overmuch, excessively.
22. to suffer, endure, permit.

Latin - 6

Across

2. of course, undoubtedly, certainly.
5. to attack, disquiet.
6. muscular, powerful.
9. to make bloody, stain with blood.
10. prior.
12. eloquence
13. a wise man, philosopher.
16. inheritance.
17. when.
18. a form, figure, after the fashion of, like.
19. rushing, seething, burning, parched; a torrent.
20. in troops, or crowds.
21. to confine, shut up, close, blockade, besiege.

Down

1. interchanged, mutually
2. not to exist.
3. to oppress, burden, make suffer.
4. complaining, whining, lamenting.
7. of the morrow, the morrow.
8. to deny; deny a debt
10. it is agreed, it is resolved, it seems good.
11. bond, fetter, tie.
14. to use abusive language; use a word incorrectly.
15. to decide, determine, settle.

Latin - 7

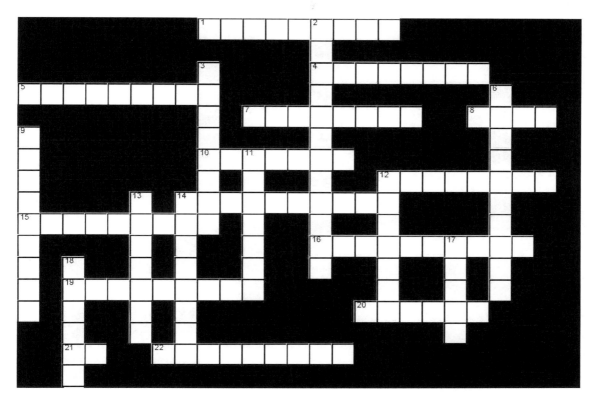

Across

1. of course, to be sure.
4. to gather together, assemble, convene.
5. advisor, counselor.
7. to revoke, render impossible, make void, annul.
8. toward, about.
10. to dig in, bury.
12. to wipe off, clean away.
14. difficult, hard, troublesome.
15. plundering, taking booty.
16. negative, containing a no, rejection.
19. to cancel, blot out.
20. afterwards.
21. to go, advance, proceed, travel, move along, progress.
22. very clever, exceedingly sharp.

Down

2. incredible, unbelievable.
3. to lure forth, entice.
6. to go forth, advance, proceed, go out.
9. mons.
11. to be failed by, disappointed by something.
12. to look at, behold, gaze at, see.
13. disgust, weariness, boredom.
14. riches, wealth.
17. the one ... the other.
18. fetters, shackles, chained.

Latin - 8

Across

3. to trip up.
5. to draw back, set aside, take away.
8. river.
10. to be an informant.
12. proficiscor : to start forward, set out, depart, arise.
14. thirty.
18. inferior, bad, wicked, persistent, perverse, bold.
19. to miss, want; seek to know.
20. day
21. pupil of the eye.
22. impudent, shameless, insolent, presumptuous.
23. by stealth, stealthily.

Down

1. file, polishing, revision.
2. chief noble, prince.
4. full, complete, full, satisfied, rich, mature, plump.
5. to ask for, look for, demand, desire, miss.
6. to exult, be joyful.
7. an enemy of the state.
9. blandishments, attractions, allurement, charm.
11. trial, attempt, essay.
12. palm.
13. to prick, sting, jab.
15. heavy, weighty, serious, important.
16. never.
17. world, universe.

Latin - 9

Across

3. to begin to shine, grow sleek.
6. on good authority.
8. prep. with abl. as far as, up to, to, down to.
10. unaccustomed; unusual, strange, uncommon.
11. distance, remoteness, isolation.
12. lamentable, deplorable, woeful.
13. majesty, dignity, greatness.
15. martial, military, war-like.
17. furniture, apparatus, gear.
18. luxuriously, delicately, slowly.
20. to rebuke, chide, scold.
21. permanency.
22. ripe beforehand, premature.
23. sacrilegious, impious.

Down

1. perjury, oath-breaking, forswearing an oath.
2. to accuse, blame, find fault with.
4. exertion, effort; undertaking.
5. crookedness, depravity, deformity, perversity.
7. former, venerable, ancient.
9. place, location, situation, spot.
12. noose, halter, snare, trap.
14. on the spot, immediately.
16. sudden, unexpected.
19. complete, finish, determine, decide, settle.

Latin - 10

Across

1. to bring or reduce to a condition, lessen.
5. joy, delight, happiness.
9. bad, wicked, evil.
10. dictator.
11. to announce, report, relate.
15. a little box, casket.
17. anjou.
18. leaden, made of lead; dull, stupid, heavy, oppressive, bad.
19. heavenly, celestial; noun, a god, dweller in heaven.
20. opportune, fit, convenient, suitable.
22. theme, title, epigram.
24. clear, bright; renowned, famous, illustrious

Down

2. to dedicate.
3. wherefore? why? for which reason.
4. speed, haste.
6. leuze.
7. sky, heaven.
8. man, hero, man of courage.
12. restrict, define, close, set a limit to.
13. to sell formally, turn over, give into charge.
14. to be born, spring forth.
15. very strong.
16. somewhat more, rather more.
21. mark, token, note, sign.
23. me

Latin - 11

Across

1. womb
3. in front of, before; on behalf of, for.
8. clean, neat, elegant.
9. to beg by entreaty, to excuse oneself; curse.
12. to ruin, destroy, bury.
17. unjust, inequitable, unfair.
19. to harass, attack.
20. difficulty, need, trouble, distress.
22. prayer, wish, desire; promise to god.
23. hedge, fence, enclosure, haye.

Down

2. plowshare.
3. to produce, disclose, bring forth.
4. repeatedly, often, one after the other, time after time.
5. to persist, persevere, continue.
6. faithlessness, disloyalty.
7. kindness, culture, refinement.
10. confine, restrain, hold back, repress.
11. spectacle, show.
13. golden.
14. end, limit, boundary, purpose.
15. to intermingle, join, mix.
16. window.
18. to be unwilling, wish not to, refuse.
19. foolish, silly; unlucky, unpropitious.
21. to calculate, count, reckon, esteem, considered.

Latin - 12

Across

1. retribution.
5. rationally, sensibly, really, indeed, to be sure.
10. to follow, trail.
13. false, deceptive.
14. wretched, unfortunate, miserable.
15. to come upon, find, discover.
16. at that time, formerly, once, for a long time now.
18. uncertain, doubtful, unsure, hesitant.
19. to direct, try, attempt, stretch, extend, present, give.
21. founder of a family, ancestor.

Down

2. angry, wrathful.
3. bad deed, crime, villainy; deed, action.
4. to take or lay hold of, receive, take in.
6. to walk.
7. i take annoyance.
8. hailstorm.
9. guiltless, innocent.
11. to train, cultivate, keep at work, exercise, practice.
12. to happen to mention.
14. wretchedly, miserably.
15. to order, command.
17. witch, vampire.
20. be made, be done, become.
21. because of, on account of.

Latin - 13

Across

1. you say.
7. door.
8. to squeeze, press down, strike down.
9. to stink, be redolent, smell bad.
10. earth, ground, land, country, soil.
16. complaint, a charge in court.
18. mourning, grief, sorrow.
19. to satisfy, sate.
21. ghosts, phantoms.
22. game, sport, school.
23. up to the time when, until, as long as, while.

Down

2. messenger, message.
3. to go off to, betake oneself to, pour forth, inflict.
4. to make known, say, speak, narrate.
5. brother.
6. slowly, calmly, cooly, deliberately.
8. to disturb, trouble, perturb, disrupt.
11. some, several.
12. of what kind? of the kind that.
13. assembly, society, union.
14. how much?
15. to attend, wait upon, assist.
17. divine law or command; fate, destiny; lawful, allowed.
18. mind, thought, intention, intellect.
20. to proclaim, make publicly known, announce, disclose.

Latin - 14

Across

1. to avoid.
4. certainly, assuredly.
6. plague, epidemic, pestilence; destruction, curse.
11. to acquire, gain, get, obtain.
14. to witness, bear witness.
15. a hinderance.
17. uncorrupted, genuine, pure.
20. great-grandson
21. linen, napkin.
23. to be absent, be away, be missing.
24. nine.
25. before, formerly.

Down

2. to kill cruelly, slay, butcher.
3. legal.
5. few, a few, some.
7. to bear, bring forth, produce; create, make, get.
8. warm, luke-warm, tepid
9. to press together, reduce, abridged.
10. faultlessness, perfection.
12. to add together, sum up, complete.
13. dream, fancy, day-dream; foolishness, nonsense.
16. overlook, despise, look down upon.
18. to send back word.
19. to promise, offer.
22. the common people, the masses, the crowd.

Latin - 15

Across

1. how, in what manner.
4. more shortly.
10. fierce, wild, savage, untamed.
12. measures, capacity.
14. bed-chamber servant, chamberlain.
17. taking by force, seizure.
18. strike, hit, hurt, damage, offend, annoy, violate.
19. to strive, exert oneself, make an effort, persevere.
20. to send, dispatch.
22. crafty, cunning, sly, deceitful.
23. to show, make clear, attempt to show.

Down

2. terrible, cruel, horror.
3. pity, mercy.
5. badly, ill, wrongly.
6. back, rear.
7. look to the interests of; consult, ask advice.
8. indignation.
9. woe, alas, woe to.
11. to cause to stand, establish, place, set up.
13. plunder, booty, spoils of war, loot, gain, prey.
14. to call together, convene.
15. bundle, pack, burden, load.
16. immediately, at once.
21. to be, exist.
24. king.

Latin - 16

Across

2. pertaining to an estate, overseer, steward.
5. beauty, grace.
8. to finish.
10. time.
12. an embracing, surrounding, loving embrace,
15. seducer.
18. beating, blow, push, impulse, influence.
20. a vineyard planted with trees.
22. uneasiness, anxiety, disquiet, apprehension.
23. to break up, dismiss, leave, abandon.
24. to sacrifice, suit, help, be of service.

Down

1. boldly, proudly, fearlessly.
2. to feed, to eat.
3. health, safety, well-being, salvation.
4. one's own, special, characteristic, particular.
6. raging, furious.
7. moderation, self-control, temperance.
9. fisherman.
11. hazardous, dangerous.
13. similar, like, equal.
14. change, alteration.
16. to be able.
17. last will, testament.
19. log, stump, tree trunk, branch, post, club.
21. to soften, make pliant.

Latin - 17

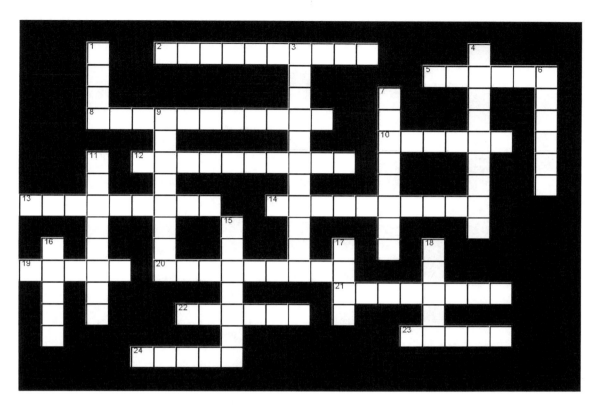

Across

2. authority
5. shortened; mutilated, defective; gelded.
8. faithlessly, disloyally.
10. entrance, door.
12. all-powerful, almighty, omnipotent
13. of today.
14. chartres.
19. to flee; interpret, understand; upset, overthrow.
20. succeeding, succession, descent, descendant.
21. to shake, disturb, agitate.
22. to respect, fear, be in dread of, to be afraid.
23. to slip, glide, slide.
24. theme.

Down

1. me
3. hardened by age, of long-standing.
4. inundation; scouring; discharge.
6. to dream; to dream of, imagine foolishly.
7. prepared, resolute, prompt.
9. foul, impure.
11. first, for the first time.
15. lizard.
16. to keep on, persist, persevere, endure.
17. passages in literary works.
18. more numerous, several, many.

Latin - 18

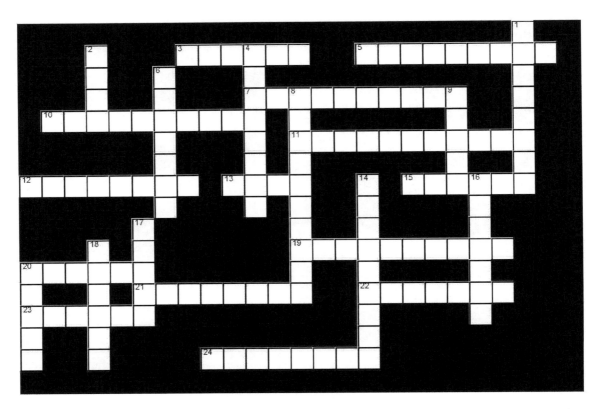

Across

3. made of copper or bronze, brazen.
5. to pollute, infect.
7. troubled, anxious, concerned, worried.
10. to throw oneself down, abase oneself.
11. fatal deadly, destructive, lethal.
12. profit, a source of profit, gaining, getting.
13. hour, time.
15. to be unsure, uncertain, wavering.
19. weeping, wailing, lamenting.
20. absent, missing, away, gone.
21. a touch, contact.
22. border, edge, extent; going around, circuit.
23. to mock, cheat.
24. health. good health, bad health.

Down

1. to grow in or on.
2. to fit, adapt, adjust, make ready, or fit.
4. to maintain, keep up, carry out, fulfill, accomplish.
6. anything made or reed -- pen, arrow, pipe, etc.
8. joyous, glad.
9. small coin, gift.
14. to disclose, expose, open, make open.
16. hated, hateful.
17. to become acquainted with, get to know.
18. to lad out colonists, found a colony.
20. to hear, hearken, listen to.

Latin - 19

Across
2. family, household.
4. to flee, retreat, run away.
6. to fish out, find out, discover.
10. faithful, loyal, true
11. forty.
13. war.
14. down from, from, concerning, about.
15. nevertheless.
18. air, atmosphere, ether, weather.
19. stiffness, hardness, sternness.
21. to choose, prefer.
22. claim, arrogate, assume, appropriate.
23. to study, pursue eagerly, be eager for.
24. theologian.

Down
1. theater.
3. a sharp point, edge, dagger point.
5. to look back, provide for, respect, have regard for.
7. a slipping or sliding.
8. language, tongue, speech.
9. to establish, cause, occasion.
11. wherefore.
12. to keep from, refrain from.
16. : a thrower, javelin man, spear thrower.
17. second.
20. to love, like, be fond of, cherish.

Latin - 20

Across

1. to hold, keep, possess, maintain.
5. non solum ... sed etiam : not only ... but also.
8. just as if.
9. to lift, raise.
11. to twist, distort.
13. embrace, grasp.
14. insane, mad, out of one's mind, foolish.
16. unexplainable, inexplicable.
17. to let go forward, send forth, promise, undertake.
18. let down, lowered, gentle, mild.
22. beautiful, handsome, fine.
23. a loan.
24. the world, the earth.

Down

2. to boil up, bubble up, to appear, produce in abundance.
3. to wonder.
4. to think meanly of, despise, condemn, hate.
6. fitness, suitability, convenience, advantage.
7. to come back, return.
8. past.
10. to support, strengthen, uphold; to besiege, oppress.
12. perhaps, probably.
15. bill of a bird, beak.
19. use, experience, skill, advantage.
20. to know.
21. but; and indeed, what is more.

Latin - 21

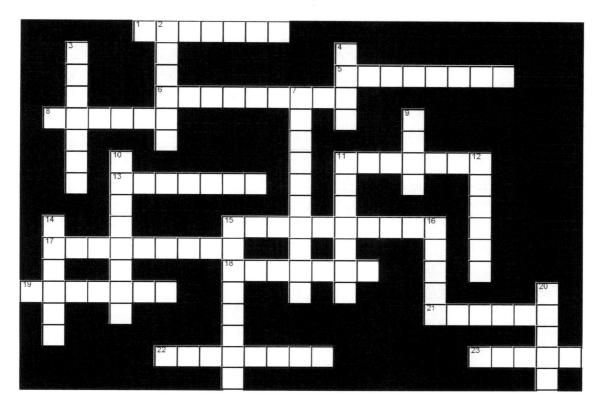

Across

1. to delay, postpone; to differ, be different.
5. exile, banishment.
6. indulgence, pliancy, submission.
8. victor, winner.
11. falling headlong.
13. to kindle, illuminate, inflame.
15. guard, garrison, detachment; protection.
17. to gather strength, become stronger.
18. to stir up, arouse, excite.
19. to press down, depress, low-lying.
21. to give a ruling, make an arrangement, decide.
22. declare, give notice, announce.
23. boundaries, limits,; territory.

Down

2. to be ignorant of, not know; rarely: neglect, overlook.
3. cheapness, low-price, worthlessness.
4. no one, nobody.
7. to come to a boil, become hot.
9. now, at the present time.
10. enticement, come-on.
11. to entrust, commit.
12. piles, heaps, masses.
14. confident, without fear, courageous.
15. subsequent, following, next, future.
16. measure, bound, limit; manner, method, mode, way.
20. to do harm to, inflict injury, hurt.

Latin - 22

Across

5. to spread, publish, impart, make accessible.
6. to seek again, ask back.
10. wisely, discreetly.
12. to break up, destroy, annihilate; spoil, weaken.
13. to magnify, glorify, honor; slay, fight, punish, afflict.
14. clever, skillful.
15. in a hostile manner, belligerently.
16. dear, beloved; costly, high-priced, expensive.
18. to approach, visit, come to, undertake.
19. a moment, crisis.
21. to announce, declare.
22. wind, rumor, favor.

Down

1. near, nearly, not far from, just now, closely.
2. rotten, decayed, putrid; loose, crumbling; flabby.
3. storm, tempest, gale.
4. hand, band, handwriting.
6. recollection, memory, recall.
7. forward, straight ahead, to sum up, utterly, wholly.
8. the godfather of a man's child.
9. rather, preferably.
10. to act a part.
11. necessary, needed, essential.
16. calamity, misfortune, disaster.
17. pearl barley, barley groats.
20. cave, cavern, grotto, den.

Latin - 23

Across

5. to drink up, suck in.
11. log, tree-trunk, branch, post, club, blockhead.
13. to lay out, expand, weigh out.
15. rouen.
16. to complain excessively, whine, gripe.
19. uproar, disturbance; mob, crowd, multitude.
20. light, slight, trivial; beardless, bald; light-armed.
21. close to, near to; just before.
22. to examine, inquire, learn.
23. to run back and forth.

Down

1. steady, firm, unchanging, constant, unwavering.
2. industry, diligence.
3. to depart, deviate, digress.
4. benefit, favor, service, privilege, right.
5. civil, civic.
6. be moderate, control oneself.
7. simple, unaffected.
8. preferring.
9. crossroads, place where four roads meet.
10. i say.
12. casting lots, deciding by lot.
14. midday, afternoon, south.
17. to make bright or clear, make clear in the mind.
18. rank, class, order.

Latin - 24

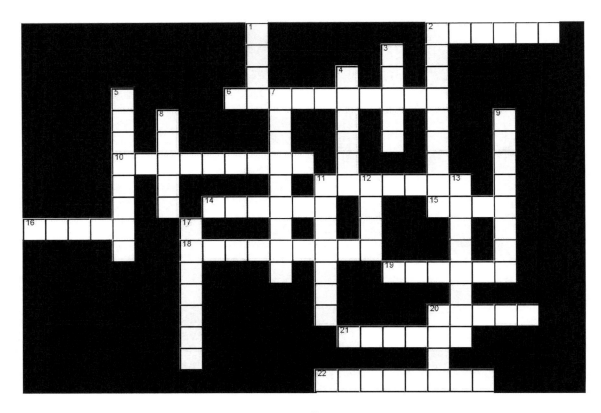

Across

2. hastily, quickly, rapidly.
6. fortunate, lucky, happy.
10. some
11. people, the people, nation, crowd, multitude, host.
14. to give orders, command; to rule, hold sway.
15. punish, fine, mulct.
16. to seize, snatch, carry away.
18. army.
19. missing letters, words, or phrases in a manuscript.
20. to tremble, shake, shudder.
21. to wipe, scour, clean
22. synagogue.

Down

1. to fly, speed, move rapidly.
2. deliberation, consultation, assembly, council.
3. enough, sufficient; sufficiently.
4. to carry in, put or place on.
5. to flatter, caress, coax.
7. to rest.
8. to sing.
9. victory.
11. to ask.
12. dutiful, godly, holy, upright, kind, honest, affectionate.
13. to run up under; aid, assist, help.
17. to wander through, travel through.
20. to cover, bury, conceal, hide, protect, shield.

Latin - 25

Across

2. decree.
5. frantic, inspired, thunder-struck, stunned.
7. in what manner, how; in whatever way, somehow.
8. to uncover, lay bare, disclose.
9. alleviation, mitigation, solace.
10. moon.
13. to bring in, introduce, import; bring upon, cause.
15. countryman, peasant, pagan.
16. to deprive
18. to adhere, stick together
19. to separate, tear apart; pillage, devastate, lay waste.
20. litter, bier.
21. to rejoice, be joyful.
22. planted with trees.

Down

1. teacher.
3. order, decree, mandate, instruction.
4. to promise to god, vow, pray for.
6. land, country, soil, ground; bottom, floor, foundation.
8. to distinguish, recognize as different.
11. in some direction.
12. to have the benefit of, to enjoy.
13. perpetual, continuous.
14. till then, till now, still, even now, besides, also, yet.
15. forward, further, next, in turn.
17. to hang to, stick to, adhere.

Latin - 26

Across

1. just short of.
3. not yet
4. to entice, allure.
8. so many.
12. easily.
14. mason
15. rotten, decayed.
16. by name, expressly.
17. across.
19. opinion, report, rumor, conjecture, report.
21. to scorn, despise, spurn.

Down

1. impenetrable.
2. harshness, bitterness.
5. to keep in, surround, contain, confine, include.
6. to pass time, live.
7. month.
9. truth.
10. to shut up, enclose.
11. to laugh at, mock, deride.
12. supporter.
13. dung, dirt, filth, manure.
14. cultivation
18. by chance, by luck, accidentally.
20. work, labor, work done, completed work, building.

Latin - 27

Across

3. to come, arrive, reach.
4. one who provides for, or against.
7. placed near, approaching, appropriate, appositively.
9. at a higher price, of a great value
12. lucky, fortunate, happy.
13. perseverance, persistence.
14. to imitate.
16. letter, epistle, missive, note; literature.
17. to commit, entrust, order, command.
20. worse.
21. to ascend, mount, go up.
22. to goad, incite, stimulate, urge.

Down

1. a biting, bite, also, sting, pain.
2. to press heavily upon, weigh down, oppress.
5. beauty, fineness.
6. longer, too long.
7. to draw together, tighten, bind.
8. destructively, injuriously.
9. openly, publicly, in the presence of.
10. luxuriously.
11. transparent, bright, clear, evident.
13. exceedingly high.
15. to seize, snatch, grasp, detain, arrest.
18. dark.
19. to instruct, teach, tutor.

Latin - 28

Across

4. to help, aid, assist.
5. profitable, gainful.
6. willingly, of one's own accord, unaided.
10. to repeat, recite, represent, imitate, pay up, deliver.
11. favorable moment, opportunity.
13. low down.
15. child, offspring.
17. weaver.
18. wide, broad, long; willing, obliging, favorable.
22. to go before, precede; to say in advance.
23. slyly, deceitfully.

Down

1. not any, no, none.
2. city.
3. fortress.
4. to go to, approach, address, attack.
7. to come near, draw near, approach.
8. advance, progress, increase.
9. take annoyance
12. thin skin, film, parchment, membrane, prepared skin.
14. to send away, let go, let slip, lose.
16. both ... and.
19. to become tired, grow weary.
20. pleasing, agreeable; grateful.
21. intensely, very much, extremely, greatly

Latin - 29

Across

2. church.
5. opportunely, conveniently.
7. to bend, incline, turn, change; fall back, waver.
8. platform, stage.
9. to prevent, hinder, restrain, prohibit, forbid.
10. to be above, have the upper hand, surpass, conquer, overcome.
13. laboriously, with great effort
17. redeemer.
19. unclean, impure, dirty, foul.
20. to create, make.
21. bind, oblige,.
22. neck.
23. huy, belgium, between liege and namur.

Down

1. ancient, old, hoary,
3. to take an oath together, plot, conspire.
4. to require, need, stand in need of.
6. to repay, reward.
9. long, stretching.
10. uneasy, worried, anxious, restless, agitated.
11. to bear, suffer, endure.
12. to disturb, upset, throw into disorder, confuse, unsettle.
14. to carry off, take away.
15. dearness, affection; charity.
16. trial, legal investigation, judgement, decision.
18. to sleep, slumber, siesta, nap.

Latin - 30

Across

1. to sift.
7. circle, orb.
8. wisdom.
11. to draw together, collect, assemble, carry out.
12. otherwise, not so.
13. to tear in pieces.
14. sickness, illness.
15. to lead through, conduct, carry through.
16. to put after, consider secondary.
17. modesty, bashfulness.
19. judgment, decision, opinion, trial
20. voyage, navigation.
22. some times.
23. to read aloud, recite.

Down

2. to return to, begin again, deduce, recall, recollect.
3. single, separate, one at a time, one each.
4. to fail, to weaken, to be in want.
5. to spare, refrain from injuring.
6. to be like, equal; make level or even, relate.
9. to blush, grow red, be ashamed.
10. to be accustomed, be used to.
14. maidservant, also used by nuns to describe themselves.
18. to carry off, to take away.
21. to carry away, remove.

Latin - 31

Across

2. to exceed, leave, pass beyond.
7. preliminary exercise, prelude.
11. price, value, reward.
13. why, wherefore.
14. butcher, slaughter-house.
18. to pity.
20. oath.
21. truce, armistice, suspension of hostilities.
23. because.
24. to carry, bear about.
25. old, aged, old man.

Down

1. again and again, repeatedly.
3. to happen, befall.
4. barley.
5. five hundred.
6. dart, javelin.
8. orphan, ward.
9. to continue, proceed, go on with.
10. northeast by north wind.
12. mild, soft, gentle.
15. to them themselves.
16. doctrine, teaching, instruction, learning.
17. cut up, broken, brief, concise.
19. following, attending, pursuing.
22. more, to a greater extent, rather, for preference

Latin - 32

Across

3. servant.
4. today.
5. to take one's stand, stand still, stop, be posted.
6. partly; some.
8. sound, healthy, sane.
9. modest. chaste.
12. to obtain, get, acquire.
14. chiefly, especially, particularly.
17. avenging, punishment, revenge.
18. to be seen, seem, appear.
21. cold, coolness, cold of winter; dullness, indolence.
22. commander in chief, general, emperor.
23. to set in mortion, impel, urge on.

Down

1. eagerly, earnestly.
2. customary, usual.
3. fortune, luck, fate, chance.
7. honey.
8. humbly, softly, calmly, modestly.
10. to intercept
11. porter, pall-bearer, carrier of a burden.
13. judgment, case; plea, litigation; defense.
15. mother.
16. nothingness, worthlessness, vanity.
19. thing, matter, business, affair.
20. to lead, induce, persuade.

Latin - 33

Across

1. to fight.
3. as soon as.
4. the left hand, left side, left-handed.
6. mortal.
9. chartres.
11. train, retinue
13. to covet, aim at, desire eagerly.
14. by no means, not at all.
15. stupid, slow, dull.
16. newness, novelty, strangeness.
19. talk, common talk, rumor
20. farm, field, acre.
21. to set over, prefer.
22. different, unlike, opposed, hostile.

Down

2. on the way, in the way; towards, against.
5. vicious, full of vice, corrupt.
7. unequal, unjust, unfair.
8. to renew, repeat, resume.
10. to charm, influence, mislead, draw in.
11. to depend on, rely on.
12. to shake violently, shake to pieces, break, shatter..
17. greedy, avaricious.
18. to make for, go to, seek, strive after.

Latin - 34

Across

3. to go out, come out.
7. most luxuriantly, most abundantly
8. disturbance, confusion.
11. unexpected, unlooked for, unanticipated.
13. from all sides, everywhere
14. put in peril, endangered.
15. to bring up, supply, provide, add
17. to bring news, report.
18. a tearing, mangling.
19. to destroy, ruin, waste, scatter, squander.
20. to set up, place
21. favorer, promoter, patron, partisan, supporter.
22. hypocrite

Down

1. smoothness, gentleness, mildness.
2. ambition, avarice
4. rhetorician, teacher of rhetoric.
5. a thousand.
6. to strike hard, pierce
9. forgetfulness, oblivion.
10. to remain, stay, stay the night
12. to use, employ, possess, enjoy.
14. to cut short, lop, mutilate.
16. always, ever.

Latin - 35

Across

1. indiscriminately.
2. school; elite troop of soldiers.
5. combined in one, whole, entire.
7. to be strong, have power, be well.
10. to remember, recollect.
12. to set free, deliver, liberate, release; exempt
13. to be unlike one's kind, fall off, degenerate.
14. silver, money.
16. countess.
18. case, envelope, covering.
20. to care for, trouble about, pay attention to.
22. quickly, rapidly, speedily.
23. to play the fool, to trifle.
24. of any kind whatever, any whatever.

Down

1. beggardry, poverty, humble circumstances.
3. shave, shear, clip, mow, reap, browse.
4. to chide, rebuke.
6. to struggle against, resist.
8. weeping, wailing.
9. partner, comrade, associate, ally, fellow.
11. to cool, grow lukewarm, decrease.
15. by the roots, utterly.
17. bending, curving.
19. cross.
21. deed, accomplishment, work, act, achievement.

Latin - 36

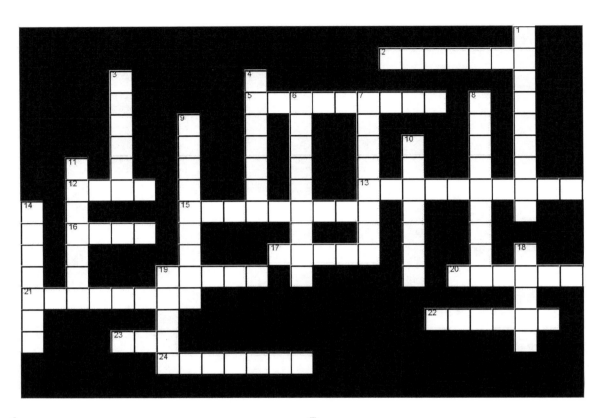

Across

2. to loiter, linger, tarry, belay.
5. repetition.
12. alquod: some.
13. proof, evidence.
15. pastry, cookie.
16. sheep.
17. to get up arise.
19. grandson.
20. especially, particularly, principally.
21. to follow, pursue, assail, reproach, rebuke, attack.
22. to fall to the ground, sink down; be ruined, destroyed.
23. adv. a long while, long time, for a long time.
24. to separate.

Down

1. brabant.
3. to set against, oppose, be opposite.
4. ancient, antique, former, old days, venerable.
6. danger, risk.
7. to set on fire, inflame, to torch, kindle.
8. patience, suffering, endurance.
9. happily.
10. corner, niche.
11. canon, member of a cathedral chapter or canonry, augustinian.
14. quitely, gently.
18. food for men and animals.
19. novel, unusual, extraordinary; news, novelty, a new thing

Latin - 37

Across

5. to say often, reiterate.
6. to accustom, acclimate, become used to.
10. to cut into.
11. otherwise, moreover, but.
13. sad-sounding, mournful, baleful.
15. virtue, right
16. character, intellect, memory, consciousness, often mind.
18. coming together, assembly, union, congress.
19. beyond, outside.
20. nearest, closest, next.
21. beard, whiskers.
22. leg, shank, shin, also foot.

Down

1. helmet.
2. to give permission; to experience, suffer.
3. strong, mighty, powerful, exceeding.
4. investigate, ask, inquire; vote, ordain, resolve.
5. anew, again, a second time, afresh.
6. rottenness, corruption, decay.
7. serious, grave, solemn.
8. into, toward, against.
9. workshop, factor.
12. as, just as, like as, just as if.
14. to wish well, greet, visit, reverence, pay respect to.
17. heart, breast.
18. carbon, coal, charcoal.

Latin - 38

Across

1. uncommonness, excellence.
6. to be angry, to be wrathful.
8. creature, servant.
9. to praise, extoll, commend; name, mention, cite, quote.
12. quiet, still, gentle.
14. fugitive : deserter, runaway slave.
15. firm, resolved, staunch.
16. agreement, contract, covenant, pact.
17. wandering, vagrant, itinerant.
21. within.
22. to carry out, bring forth.
23. careful, attentive; curious, inquisitive; worn out by cares.

Down

2. triumphal procession, triumph.
3. to give a nod to, give a sign to.
4. a thousand times.
5. talk, report, rumor, tradition.
7. to refuse.
10. put before, prefer, favor, promote.
11. get the start of.
12. to carry on, carry forward, advance, promote,
13. those down below, the dead.
14. to occupy oneself, perform, do, execute.
18. gain, profit.
19. pure, free from.
20. to destroy, wipe out, erase.

Latin - 39

Across

1. anyone, anything.
3. to draw out, draw on, produce, recall to the colors.
5. plainly, clearly.
6. diligent, careful.
9. to prevail upon a person, entreat successfully.
10. outermost, last, extreme.
15. courtrai.
17. sleepy, drowsy
20. before; in front of; before, previously.
22. steadily, firmly.
23. refute, disprove, contradict.

Down

2. far.
4. strained, stretched; eager, zealous.
5. to rain, shower, sprinkle.
7. ravisher, debaucher.
8. to falsify; to corrupt.
11. rustic, rural; peasant.
12. episcopal
13. in return for, instead of; for, as.
14. deadly, lethal.
15. delayer, procrastinator,
16. power to command, authority, command, rule, control.
18. to become soft, flexible, sticky; to weaken, slacken.
19. to rush in, fling in.
21. a hole, empty space; pond, pool; deficiency, loss.

Latin - 40

Across

1. how great?
3. court
5. to strike, beat; bewail, mourn.
6. to drive away, thrust out.
8. to return, come back.
11. precept.
13. so often, so many times.
14. forehead, brow, front.
15. up to, down to as far as.
16. alone, only, the only.
18. to make a bargain or agreement, covenant, deal.
20. to declare, announce, report, give notice.
21. not.
22. to become bright again.
23. board, plank, gaming board, painted panel.

Down

2. fright, fear, terror.
4. to strike, hit, knock; cause damage.
7. completion, summing up, adding up.
9. to reflect upon, consider, ponder; practice.
10. after.
11. to be punished.
12. pattern, model, example .
16. sharing, associated, allied.
17. maiden, virgin, young girl.
19. in one, together.

Latin - 41

Across

3. corbie.
6. knowledge, science, skill.
9. undecided, void, unfixed, of no effect.
10. thorough, tense, anxious, strict.
11. worry, fatigue, vex, harass, tease.
13. wetness, moisture.
15. to wander, stray, rove; be mistaken, err, go astray.
17. to shorten, abbreviate.
18. new, fresh, young, inexperienced, revived, refreshed.
19. wicked, accursed, infamous, criminal.
20. stuffed full, crammed, jammed.
21. feeling, sense.

Down

1. to chirp, tweet, pipe.
2. to act foolishly, play the fool, make an ass of one's self.
4. to implore, entreat, beg, call as a witness.
5. beautiful, pretty, charming, handsome.
7. notice sent to a higher tribunal.
8. to hasten; accelerate, speed up.
12. ground, earth, soil; land, country.
14. ninth.
15. even, also.
16. sword.
17. all, all collectively, the whole.

Latin - 42

Across

1. beautifully, finely, handsomely.
6. fitted, connected, fastened; prepared, fitted out.
7. to have, hold, possess; consider, regard.
10. angered, exasperated; disturbed, restless, troubled.
11. letter.
12. to enrich, make wealthy.
13. fidelity, loyalty, homage.
16. to hang over, be imminent, threaten.
18. to rush, fall, be ruined.
20. friend, comrade.
22. stubbornly, obstinately.
23. so far, thus far, up to then.
24. ordinary, undistinguished, within bounds.

Down

2. chapter, chapter meeting, chapter house.
3. rule, government, order, arrangment, regulation.
4. to grab, try to get, grab at.
5. strongly, bravely.
8. bell.
9. rhetorical attack; wounding.
13. to hasten, hurry, speed.
14. light.
15. for a long while, a long while ago, some time age.
17. deserve, earn, be entitled to, merit.
19. often, so many times.
21. be without, be deprived of, lack, want.

Latin - 43

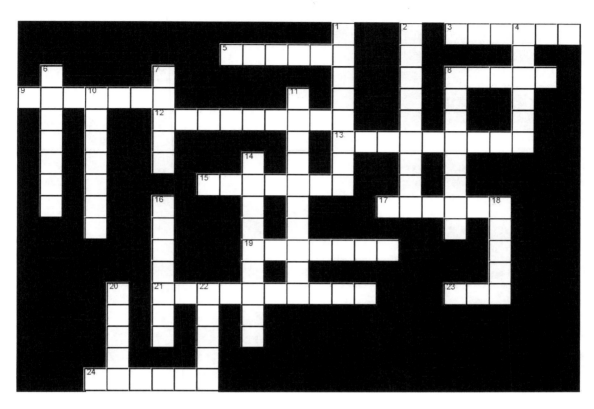

Across

3. one hundred, 100.
5. to lay to a charge, enter in an account, impute to.
8. to seize, take, choose; attack, injure; comprehend.
9. judgement.
12. ordinary, average, fair, moderate, mediocre.
13. to arrange, decide, appoint, settle, found, set up.
15. dead, deceased, passed away, gone west, departed.
17. satire.
19. to look at attentively, gaze at, consider.
21. delight, pleasure, enjoyment.
23. night.
24. chasm, pit, abyss.

Down

1. flashing, twinkling, shaking, trembling.
2. alms
4. to give out, divide, allot, assign, grant, give, allow.
6. lay up, store, hoard.
7. notwithstanding, nevertheless, yet, still, for all that.
8. hair.
10. above, upper, high.
11. a large concourse, population, numerous assembly.
14. mixed, indiscriminate; commonplace, usual.
16. continuously, without remission.
18. bold
20. to learn, become acquainted with.
22. to bend.

Latin - 44

Across

4. inventor, discoverer.
5. sad, gloomy, downcast.
7. to touch, reach, grasp, affect, infect.
8. free time, leisure, ease, peace, repose.
9. common, general, run of the mill.
13. damage, loss, detriment.
14. thence, from there, for that reason, thereafter, then.
15. a tree branch.
17. follower, pursuer.
19. cautiously, with security.
21. to seek, search for; ask, enquire, search for
22. to taste.
23. to be established, stand firm, stop, endure.

Down

1. to contend, settle, dispute, to settle by combat.
2. charming, witty, pleasant, elegant.
3. weakness, feebleness; instability, fickleness.
6. unmoved.
10. and, so, therefore.
11. to take vengeance for, avenge.
12. road, way, street.
16. to capture, overcome, subdue..
18. death.
20. to gather, choose, collect, pass through, read,

Latin - 45

Across

1. have confidence in, be confident of, rely upon.
4. a dwarf.
7. threshold.
8. defense, protection
9. agreeing, fit, suitable.
12. to draw out, protract, defer, make known.
13. to pick out, select, choose.
14. to remain behind, stay, continue.
16. thence, next; thereupon, after that, then; accordingly.
17. step-daughter.
19. to limp, halt, be lame, to hobble.
20. slave, serf.
21. from above, above.
22. grace, indulgence, favor, pardon, forgiveness.

Down

1. loud shouting, cry.
2. means, wealth, abundance, riches, resources.
3. fortifying, defense works, bridging, fortification.
5. maternal aunt.
6. to direct one's course, tend, make or head for.
10. firm, stable, steadfast.
11. to speak, argue, plead, orate, beg, entreat.
12. inside, widely, through and through, completely.
15. magical.
16. to inform fully, instruct thoroughly.
18. fame, renown, glory.

Latin - 46

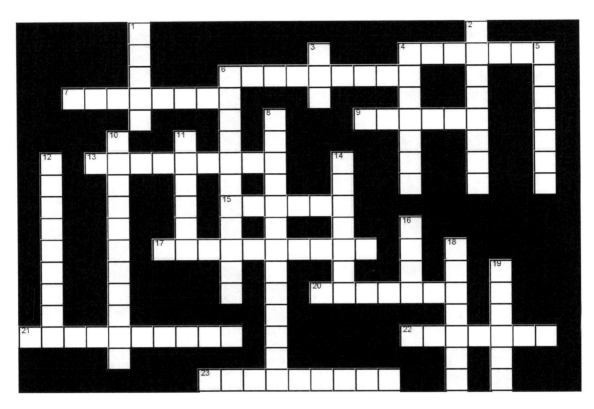

Across

4. the dead.
6. to crowd, collect in large number, visit.
7. willingly, with pleasure.
9. some.
13. foresight, wisdom, discretion.
15. star, constellation.
17. best of all, chief, principal.
20. to cover, shield, protect, defend.
21. a gathering together, a summing up, a uniting.
22. to have no hope, despair, give up.
23. cure, remedy, nostrum, medicine.

Down

1. before, previously, formerly.
2. undertaker.
3. at that time, then; thereupon, in the next place.
4. noise, sound.
5. to drive against, strike upon.
6. fruitful, fertile.
8. however great
10. rule, dominion, pre-eminence, first place.
11. to hand over, carry down, communicate, offer, refer.
12. to indicate, show, describe, explain.
14. to burn up, to ruin, consume.
16. truly, really, actually, rightly.
18. apart, separately.
19. to carry out, bury, lift up, exalt.

Latin - 47

Across

1. wine.
3. either of the two
4. to drive before one, drive away.
6. to stain, blemish, defile, pollute.
8. to turn sideways, turn aside.
9. immortal.
10. sign, seal, indication, sign.
11. welcome, pleasant, agreeable.
15. break, break open.
18. below, underneath; to the south, in the underworld.
19. no, not at all, by no means.
20. vote, franchise; approval support, aid, assistance.
21. heat, tide.
22. pain, grief. misery, pain, suffering.
23. tearful, mournful, shedding tears,

Down

2. sailor.
4. boyishly, childishly, foolishly.
5. contemptuously.
7. annoyance, troublesomeness; stiffness, affectation.
11. farm, field, acre.
12. conscious of, aware of.
13. probity, uprightness, honesty.
14. flight, escape,
16. to confess, admit, allow, reveal, make known.
17. to bend, arch, curve; influence.

Latin - 48

Across

4. to place near, put to, serve, put on the table.
10. an oak grove, and oak forest.
12. improvident, negligent
14. discuss, debate, confer; betake oneself, devote.
15. chain, fetters.
16. by much, by far, by a great deal, by a lot.
17. the elbow; a cubit.

Down

1. just as, according to.
2. to make fit, adapt, please, oblige, serve.
3. growth, enlargement, increase.
5. offspring, descendants, posterity..
6. the aristocratic party.
7. to stretch, strain, try to prove.
8. manfully.
9. wildly, savagely, fiercely, cruelly, roughly
10. square, a square.
11. to serve, wait upon, provide, supply.
13. to call into question.
14. blind, sightless.

Latin - 49

Across

6. bench, stool.
7. twice.
10. to bewail, weep for.
13. explanation, exposition.
15. to hurl, throw; put together, conjecture.
16. to weigh, value, consider, judge, esteem.
18. painter
21. accusation, calumny, charge.
23. adv. far and wide, everywhere, scattered about.
24. woman.
25. to make anew, refresh, revive, change, alter, invent.

Down

1. cat.
2. flame, fire.
3. money.
4. gradually, little by little.
5. hire, employ for wages, among many other meanings.
8. to put to shame, disgrace.
9. milky, of milk, milk-white.
11. enticement, allurement.
12. discuss.
14. filth, meanness, stinginess.
17. hold off, hold back, detain.
19. sacred precinct, temple, sometimes church.
20. ease, leisure, inactivity.
22. road, route, journey.

Latin - 50

Across

3. bread.
10. mirror.
13. fourth.
14. sobbing, death rattle.
16. hollow, basket, bed.
18. the herb thyme.
20. feel, perceive, experience, hold an opinion,
22. a nodding, nod, command, will.
23. to put down, lay aside.

Down

1. untamed, wild.
2. briefly.
4. unwilling, against one's will.
5. savagery, frightfulness.
6. fig tree.
7. pleasure.
8. carrying about, conduct .
9. which? what?
11. to drag, forcibly conduct, entice, allure.
12. crumb, morsel, grain.
13. for how much, at what price.
15. to form again, mould anew.
17. to count, estimate; prune, cut off.
19. honor, esteem, public office.
21. or

Latin - 1

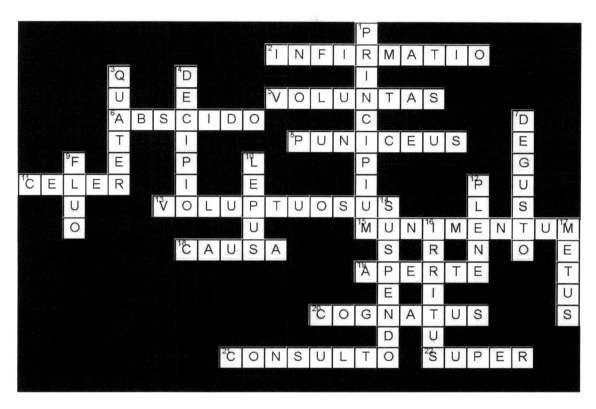

Across

2. weakening; refusing; invalidating. [INFIRMATIO]

5. wish, will, inclination. [VOLUNTAS]
6. to cut off, to separate, take away. [ABSCIDO]
8. purple, red. [PUNICEUS]
11. quick, swift, rapid, speedy, fast. [CELER]
13. delightful, pleasurable. [VOLUPTUOSUS]
15. fortification, protection, defenses. [MUNIMENTUM]
18. on account of, for the sake of. [CAUSA]
19. openly, frankly. [APERTE]
20. related by blood, kinsman. [COGNATUS]
21. to consider carefully, weigh, ponder. [CONSULTO]
22. over, above; concerning, about, besides. [SUPER]

Down

1. beginning. [PRINCIPIUM]
3. four times; again and again. [QUATER]
4. ensnare, trap, beguile, deceive, cheat. [DECIPIO]
7. to taste. [DEGUSTO]
9. to flow, pour, stream. [FLUO]
10. hare, rabbit. [LEPUS]
12. completely, wholly, fully. [PLENE]
14. to suspend, hang. [SUSPENDO]
16. vain, useless, ineffectual, of not effect. [IRRITUS]
17. fear, dread, anxiety. [METUS]

Latin - 2

Across

6. to injure, weaken, discourage, damage, break. [ADFLICTO]
8. to turn away, avert, avoid. turn back. [AVERTO]
11. to tinge, dye, stain, imbue. [INFICIO]
13. to show oneself, present oneself. [PRAEBEO]
14. to produce, engender. [PROGENERO]
16. composition, agreement, pact; arrangement. [COMPOSITIO]
18. eagerness, zeal. [STUDIUM]
19. death, ruin, annihilation. [LETUM]
21. at least, at all events. [SALTEM]
22. loveliness, charm, attractiveness, beauty. [VENUSTAS]
23. to graze, forage, browse. [PASCO]

Down

1. to punish. [PLECTO]
2. master, canon; master of a school, professor. [MAGISTER]
3. admonition, warning. [MONITIO]
4. able, mighty, powerful, strong. [POTENS]
5. to examine, treat of, discuss. [DISSERO]
7. citizen, townsman, bourgeois, burgess. [CIVIS]
9. triers. [TREVERIM]
10. to be silent, leave unmentioned. [TACEO]
12. false conclusions, logical fallacies. [SOPHISMATA]
13. at first, for the first time, in the first place. [PRIMUM]
15. violent, furious, impetuous. [VEHEMENS]
17. dark-colored, blackish [PULLUS]
20. foreign, acquired. [US]

Latin - 3

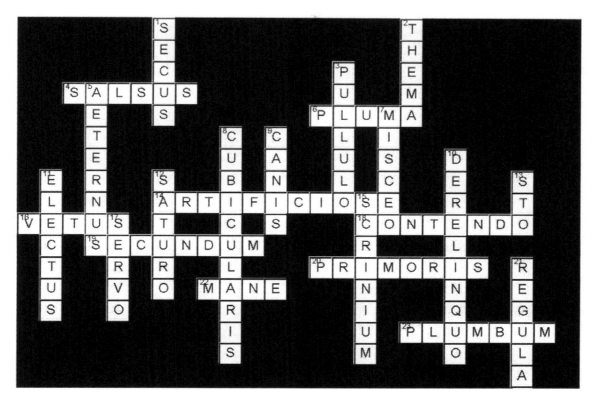

Across

4. salty, witty. [SALSUS]
6. feather; featherbed; pen. [PLUMA]
14. skillfully. [ARTIFICIOSE]
16. old. [VETUS]
18. to compare, contrast; compete. [CONTENDO]
19. after, behind. [SECUNDUM]
20. first, foremost; most distinguished, first. [PRIMORIS]
22. morning, early in the morning, early. [MANE]
23. tin. [PLUMBUM]

Down

1. differently from, otherwise than. [SECUS]
2. subject, topic, theme. [THEMA]
3. shoot up, sprout, burgeon. [PULLULO]
5. eternal, everlasting, without end. [AETERNUS]
7. to mix, mingle, blend. [MISCEO]
8. pertaining to a bedroom [CUBICULARIS]
9. dog. [CANIS]
10. to forsake, desert, abandon. [DERELINQUO]
11. chosen, select. [ELECTUS]
12. to fill, satisfy. [SATURO]
13. to stand, stand still, stand firm. [STO]
15. bookcase, case for papers. [SCRINIUM]
17. to watch over, keep, protect, observe, save, reserve. [SERVO]
21. rule; monastic rule. [REGULA]

Latin - 4

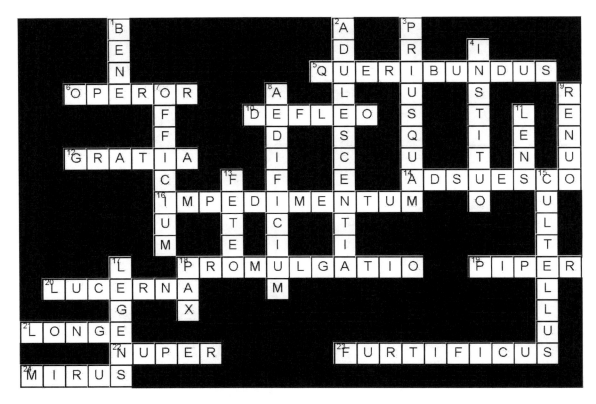

Across

5. complaining, plaintive, whining. [QUERIBUNDUS]
6. to work, labor, toil, take pains. [OPEROR]
10. to weep for, bewail. [DEFLEO]
12. in order to, for the sake of, to. [GRATIA]
14. to grow accustomed to, used to, make familiar. [ADSUESCO]
16. hindrance, impediment, obstacle, difficulty. [IMPEDIMENTUM]
18. publication, promulgation. [PROMULGATIO]
19. pepper. [PIPER]
20. lamp. [LUCERNA]
21. far and wide. [LONGE]
22. newly, recently, not long ago. [NUPER]
23. thievish. [FURTIFICUS]
24. wonderful, astonishing, extraordinary. [MIRUS]

Down

1. melior : optime : well, better, best [BENE]
2. youth [ADULESCENTIA]
3. before. [PRIUSQUAM]
4. to establish, found, institute. [INSTITUO]
7. duty, service, job. [OFFICIUM]
8. building, structure. [AEDIFICIUM]
9. to deny, refuse, reject. [RENUO]
11. lentil. [LENS]
13. to have a bad odor, stink. [FETEO]
15. a little knife. [CULTELLUS]
17. a reader. [LEGENS]
18. peace [PAX]

Latin - 5

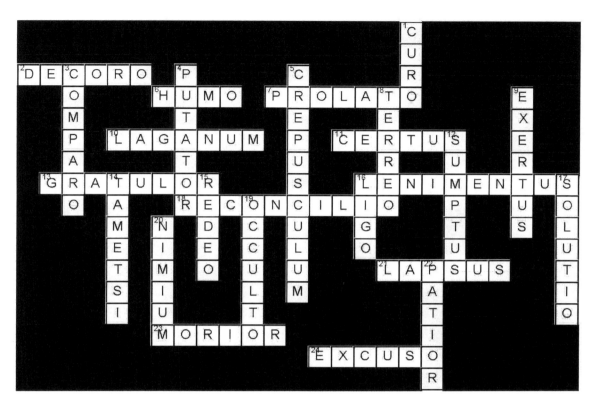

Across

2. beautify, embellish, adorn. [DECORO]
6. cover with earth, bury, [HUMO]
7. to enlarge, lengthen, extend; put off, defer. [PROLATO]
10. a cake. [LAGANUM]
11. settled, resolved, decided. [CERTUS]
13. to wish a person joy, congratulate ,give thanks [GRATULOR]
16. alleviation, improvement, mitigation. [LENIMENTUS]
18. to restore, repair; unite, reconcile. [RECONCILIO]
21. fall, fault, error, sliding, graduate movement. [LAPSUS]
23. to die, wither away, decay. [MORIOR]
24. to exempt from blame, excuse, make excuses, plead. [EXCUSO]

Down

1. manage, administer; provide money. [CURO]
3. to compare. [COMPARO]
4. pruner. [PUTATOR]
5. dusk, twilight. [CREPUSCULUM]
8. to frighten, terrify, scare away, deter. [TERREO]
9. tested, tried, approved, experienced. [EXERTUS]
12. expense, cost. [SUMPTUS]
14. even if, although. [TAMETSI]
15. to go back, come back, return; to come in. [REDEO]
16. to bind, tie. [LIGO]
17. loosening; payment. [SOLUTIO]
19. secretly. [OCCULTO]
20. too much, overmuch, excessively. [NIMIUM]
22. to suffer, endure, permit. [PATIOR]

Latin - 6

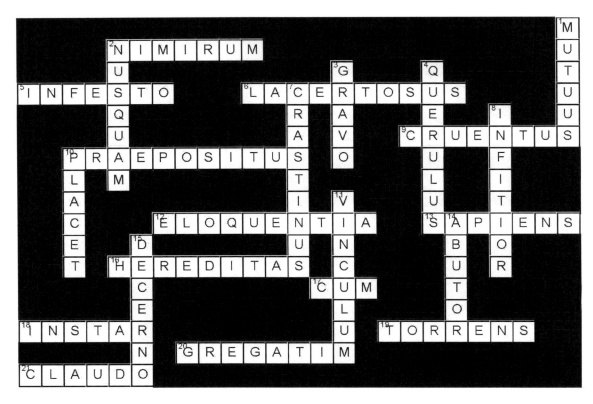

Across

2. of course, undoubtedly, certainly. [NIMIRUM]
5. to attack, disquiet. [INFESTO]
6. muscular, powerful. [LACERTOSUS]
9. to make bloody, stain with blood. [CRUENTUS]
10. prior. [PRAEPOSITUS]
12. eloquence [ELOQUENTIA]
13. a wise man, philosopher. [SAPIENS]
16. inheritance. [HEREDITAS]
17. when. [CUM]
18. a form, figure, after the fashion of, like. [INSTAR]
19. rushing, seething, burning, parched; a torrent. [TORRENS]
20. in troops, or crowds. [GREGATIM]
21. to confine, shut up, close, blockade, besiege. [CLAUDO]

Down

1. interchanged, mutually [MUTUUS]
2. not to exist. [NUSQUAM]
3. to oppress, burden, make suffer. [GRAVO]
4. complaining, whining, lamenting. [QUERULUS]

7. of the morrow, the morrow. [CRASTINUS]
8. to deny; deny a debt [INFITIOR]
10. it is agreed, it is resolved, it seems good. [PLACET]
11. bond, fetter, tie. [VINCULUM]
14. to use abusive language; use a word incorrectly. [ABUTOR]
15. to decide, determine, settle. [DECERNO]

Latin - 7

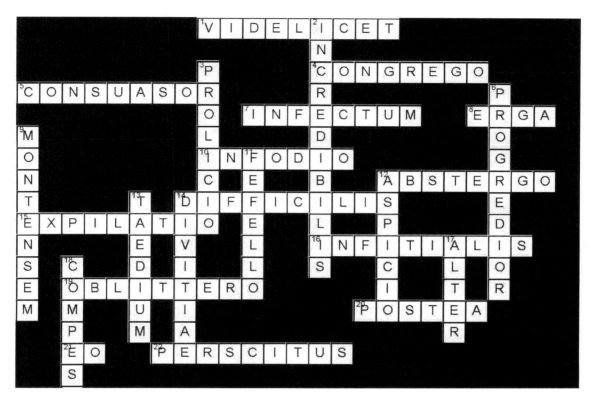

Across

1. of course, to be sure. [VIDELICET]
4. to gather together, assemble, convene. [CONGREGO]
5. advisor, counselor. [CONSUASOR]
7. to revoke, render impossible, make void, annul. [INFECTUM]
8. toward, about. [ERGA]
10. to dig in, bury. [INFODIO]
12. to wipe off, clean away. [ABSTERGO]
14. difficult, hard, troublesome. [DIFFICILIS]
15. plundering, taking booty. [EXPILATIO]
16. negative, containing a no, rejection. [INFITIALIS]

19. to cancel, blot out. [OBLITTERO]
20. afterwards. [POSTEA]
21. to go, advance, proceed, travel, move along, progress. [EO]
22. very clever, exceedingly sharp. [PERSCITUS]

Down

2. incredible, unbelievable. [INCREDIBILIS]
3. to lure forth, entice. [PROLICIO]
6. to go forth, advance, proceed, go out. [PROGREDIOR]
9. mons. [MONTENSEM]
11. to be failed by, disappointed by something. [FEFELLO]
12. to look at, behold, gaze at, see. [ASPICIO]
13. disgust, weariness, boredom. [TAEDIUM]
14. riches, wealth. [DIVITIAE]
17. the one ... the other. [ALTER]
18. fetters, shackles, chained. [COMPES]

Latin - 8

Across

3. to trip up. [SUPPLANTO]
5. to draw back, set aside, take away. [REMOVEO]

8. river. [FLUMEN]
10. to be an informant. [QUADRUPLOR]
12. proficiscor : to start forward, set out, depart, arise. [PROFICUUS]
14. thirty. [TRIGINTA]
18. inferior, bad, wicked, persistent, perverse, bold. [IMPROBUS]
19. to miss, want; seek to know. [QUAERO]
20. day [DIES]
21. pupil of the eye. [PUPULA]
22. impudent, shameless, insolent, presumptuous. [IMPUDENS]
23. by stealth, stealthily. [FURTIM]

Down

1. file, polishing, revision. [LIMA]
2. chief noble, prince. [PROCER]
4. full, complete, full, satisfied, rich, mature, plump. [PLENUS]
5. to ask for, look for, demand, desire, miss. [REQUIRO]
6. to exult, be joyful. [EXULTO]
7. an enemy of the state. [HOSTIS]
9. blandishments, attractions, allurement, charm. [BLANDITIA]
11. trial, attempt, essay. [RUDIMENTUM]
12. palm. [PALMA]
13. to prick, sting, jab. [FODIO]
15. heavy, weighty, serious, important. [GRAVIS]
16. never. [NUNQUAM]
17. world, universe. [MUNDUS]

Latin - 9

Across

3. to begin to shine, grow sleek. [NITESCO]
6. on good authority. [COMPERTE]
8. prep. with abl. as far as, up to, to, down to. [TENUS]
10. unaccustomed; unusual, strange, uncommon. [INSOLITUS]
11. distance, remoteness, isolation. [LOGINQUITAS]
12. lamentable, deplorable, woeful. [LACRIMABILIS]
13. majesty, dignity, greatness. [MAIESTAS]
15. martial, military, war-like. [BELLICUS]
17. furniture, apparatus, gear. [SUPELLEX]
18. luxuriously, delicately, slowly. [DELICATE]
20. to rebuke, chide, scold. [INCREPARE]
21. permanency. [MANENTIA]
22. ripe beforehand, premature. [PRAECOX]
23. sacrilegious, impious. [SACRILEGUS]

Down

1. perjury, oath-breaking, forswearing an oath. [PERIURIUM]
2. to accuse, blame, find fault with. [ACCUSO]
4. exertion, effort; undertaking. [CONATUS]
5. crookedness, depravity, deformity, perversity. [PRAVITAS]
7. former, venerable, ancient. [PRISTINUS]
9. place, location, situation, spot. [LOCUS]
12. noose, halter, snare, trap. [LAQUEUM]
14. on the spot, immediately. [ILICO]
16. sudden, unexpected. [SUBITUS]
19. complete, finish, determine, decide, settle. [EXIGO]

Latin - 10

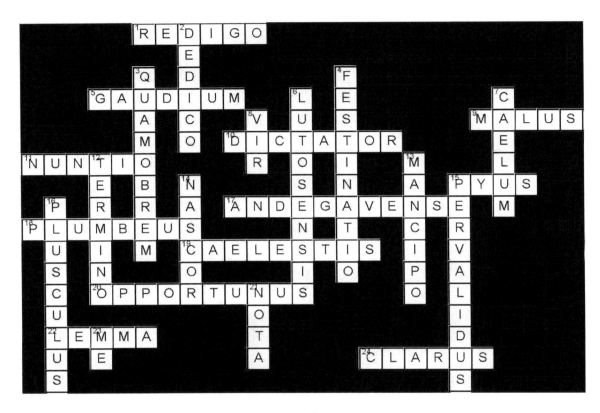

Across

1. to bring or reduce to a condition, lessen. [REDIGO]
5. joy, delight, happiness. [GAUDIUM]
9. bad, wicked, evil. [MALUS]
10. dictator. [DICTATOR]
11. to announce, report, relate. [NUNTIO]
15. a little box, casket. [PYUS]
17. anjou. [ANDEGAVENSE]
18. leaden, made of lead; dull, stupid, heavy, oppressive, bad. [PLUMBEUS]
19. heavenly, celestial; noun, a god, dweller in heaven. [CAELESTIS]
20. opportune, fit, convenient, suitable. [OPPORTUNUS]
22. theme, title, epigram. [LEMMA]
24. clear, bright; renowned, famous, illustrious [CLARUS]

Down

2. to dedicate. [DEDICO]
3. wherefore? why? for which reason. [QUAMOBREM]
4. speed, haste. [FESTINATIO]
6. leuze. [LUTOSENSIS]
7. sky, heaven. [CAELUM]
8. man, hero, man of courage. [VIR]
12. restrict, define, close, set a limit to. [TERMINO]
13. to sell formally, turn over, give into charge. [MANCIPO]
14. to be born, spring forth. [NASCOR]
15. very strong. [PERVALIDUS]
16. somewhat more, rather more. [PLUSCULUS]
21. mark, token, note, sign. [NOTA]
23. me [ME]

Latin - 11

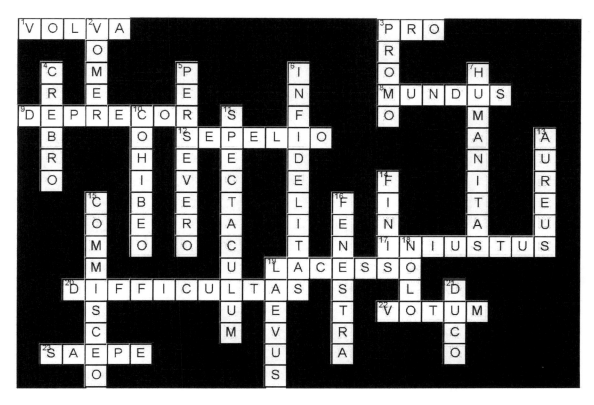

Across

1. womb [VOLVA]
3. in front of, before; on behalf of, for. [PRO]
8. clean, neat, elegant. [MUNDUS]
9. to beg by entreaty, to excuse oneself; curse. [DEPRECOR]
12. to ruin, destroy, bury. [SEPELIO]
17. unjust, inequitable, unfair. [INIUSTUS]
19. to harass, attack. [LACESSO]
20. difficulty, need, trouble, distress. [DIFFICULTAS]
22. prayer, wish, desire; promise to god. [VOTUM]
23. hedge, fence, enclosure, haye. [SAEPE]

Down

2. plowshare. [VOMER]
3. to produce, disclose, bring forth. [PROMO]
4. repeatedly, often, one after the other, time after time. [CREBRO]
5. to persist, persevere, continue. [PERSEVERO]
6. faithlessness, disloyalty. [INFIDELITAS]
7. kindness, culture, refinement. [HUMANITAS]
10. confine, restrain, hold back, repress. [COHIBEO]
11. spectacle, show. [SPECTACULUM]
13. golden. [AUREUS]
14. end, limit, boundary, purpose. [FINIS]
15. to intermingle, join, mix. [COMMISCEO]
16. window. [FENESTRA]
18. to be unwilling, wish not to, refuse. [NOLO]
19. foolish, silly; unlucky, unpropitious. [LAEVUS]
21. to calculate, count, reckon, esteem, considered. [DUCO]

Latin - 12

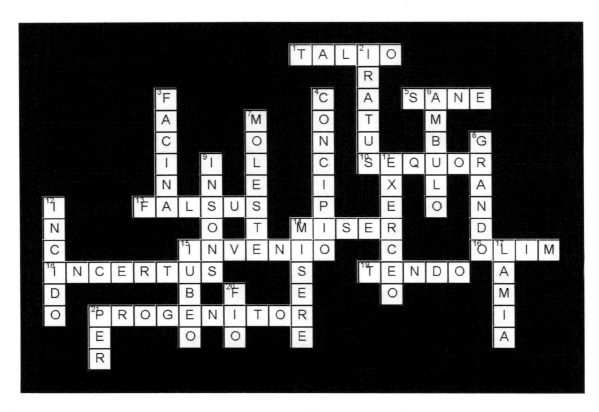

Across

1. retribution. [TALIO]
5. rationally, sensibly, really, indeed, to be sure. [SANE]
10. to follow, trail. [SEQUOR]
13. false, deceptive. [FALSUS]
14. wretched, unfortunate, miserable. [MISER]
15. to come upon, find, discover. [INVENIO]
16. at that time, formerly, once, for a long time now. [OLIM]
18. uncertain, doubtful, unsure, hesitant. [INCERTUS]
19. to direct, try, attempt, stretch, extend, present, give. [TENDO]
21. founder of a family, ancestor. [PROGENITOR]

Down

2. angry, wrathful. [IRATUS]
3. bad deed, crime, villainy; deed, action. [FACINA]
4. to take or lay hold of, receive, take in. [CONCIPIO]
6. to walk. [AMBULO]
7. i take annoyance. [MOLESTE]
8. hailstorm. [GRANDO]
9. guiltless, innocent. [INSONS]
11. to train, cultivate, keep at work, exercise, practice. [EXERCEO]
12. to happen to mention. [INCIDO]
14. wretchedly, miserably. [MISERE]
15. to order, command. [IUBEO]
17. witch, vampire. [LAMIA]
20. be made, be done, become. [FIO]
21. because of, on account of. [PER]

Latin - 13

Across

1. you say. [INQUIS]
7. door. [IANUA]
8. to squeeze, press down, strike down. [PREMO]
9. to stink, be redolent, smell bad. [PUTEO]
10. earth, ground, land, country, soil. [TERRA]
16. complaint, a charge in court. [QUERIMONIA]
18. mourning, grief, sorrow. [MAEROR]
19. to satisfy, sate. [SATIO]
21. ghosts, phantoms. [LEMURES]
22. game, sport, school. [LUDUS]
23. up to the time when, until, as long as, while. [DONEC]

Down

2. messenger, message. [NUNTIUS]
3. to go off to, betake oneself to, pour forth, inflict. [INGERO]
4. to make known, say, speak, narrate. [NARRO]
5. brother. [FRATER]
6. slowly, calmly, cooly, deliberately. [LENTE]
8. to disturb, trouble, perturb, disrupt. [PERTURBO]
11. some, several. [ALIQUOT]
12. of what kind? of the kind that. [QUALIS]
13. assembly, society, union. [CONGREGATIO]
14. how much? [QUANTUM]
15. to attend, wait upon, assist. [MINISTRO]
17. divine law or command; fate, destiny; lawful, allowed. [FAS]
18. mind, thought, intention, intellect. [MENS]
20. to proclaim, make publicly known, announce, disclose. [INDICO]

Latin - 14

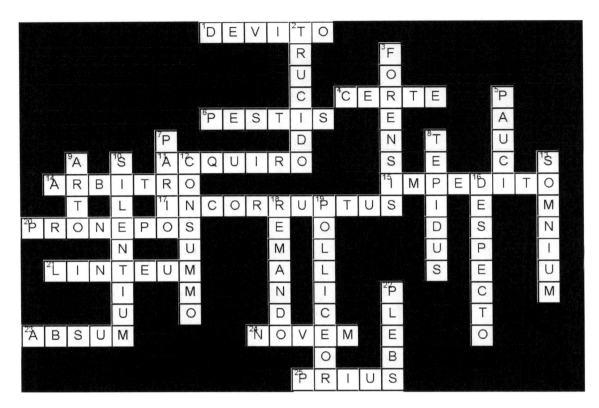

Across

1. to avoid. [DEVITO]
4. certainly, assuredly. [CERTE]
6. plague, epidemic, pestilence; destruction, curse. [PESTIS]
11. to acquire, gain, get, obtain. [ACQUIRO]
14. to witness, bear witness. [ARBITRO]
15. a hinderance. [IMPEDITO]
17. uncorrupted, genuine, pure. [INCORRUPTUS]
20. great-grandson [PRONEPOS]
21. linen, napkin. [LINTEUM]
23. to be absent, be away, be missing. [ABSUM]
24. nine. [NOVEM]
25. before, formerly. [PRIUS]

Down

2. to kill cruelly, slay, butcher. [TRUCIDO]
3. legal. [FORENSIS]
5. few, a few, some. [PAUCI]
7. to bear, bring forth, produce; create, make, get. [PARIO]
8. warm, luke-warm, tepid [TEPIDUS]
9. to press together, reduce, abridged. [ARTO]
10. faultlessness, perfection. [SILENTIUM]
12. to add together, sum up, complete. [CONSUMMO]
13. dream, fancy, day-dream; foolishness, nonsense. [SOMNIUM]
16. overlook, despise, look down upon. [DESPECTO]
18. to send back word. [REMANDO]
19. to promise, offer. [POLLICEOR]
22. the common people, the masses, the crowd. [PLEBS]

Latin - 15

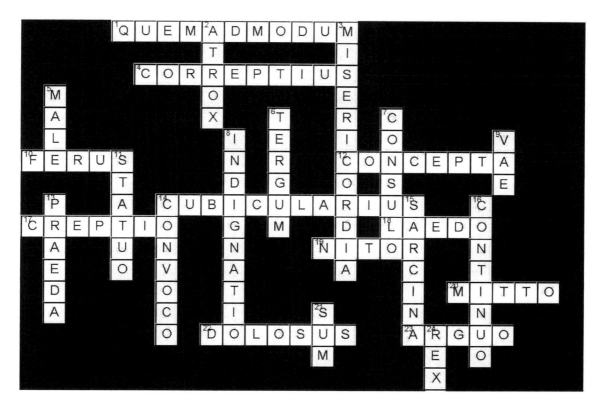

Across

1. how, in what manner. [QUEMADMODUM]
4. more shortly. [CORREPTIUS]
10. fierce, wild, savage, untamed. [FERUS]
12. measures, capacity. [CONCEPTA]
14. bed-chamber servant, chamberlain. [CUBICULARIUS]
17. taking by force, seizure. [CREPTIO]
18. strike, hit, hurt, damage, offend, annoy, violate. [LAEDO]
19. to strive, exert oneself, make an effort, persevere. [NITOR]
20. to send, dispatch. [MITTO]
22. crafty, cunning, sly, deceitful. [DOLOSUS]
23. to show, make clear, attempt to show. [ARGUO]

Down

2. terrible, cruel, horror. [ATROX]
3. pity, mercy. [MISERICORDIA]
5. badly, ill, wrongly. [MALE]
6. back, rear. [TERGUM]
7. look to the interests of; consult, ask advice. [CONSULO]
8. indignation. [INDIGNATIO]
9. woe, alas, woe to. [VAE]
11. to cause to stand, establish, place, set up. [STATUO]
13. plunder, booty, spoils of war, loot, gain, prey. [PRAEDA]
14. to call together, convene. [CONVOCO]
15. bundle, pack, burden, load. [SARCINA]
16. immediately, at once. [CONTINUO]
21. to be, exist. [SUM]
24. king. [REX]

Latin - 16

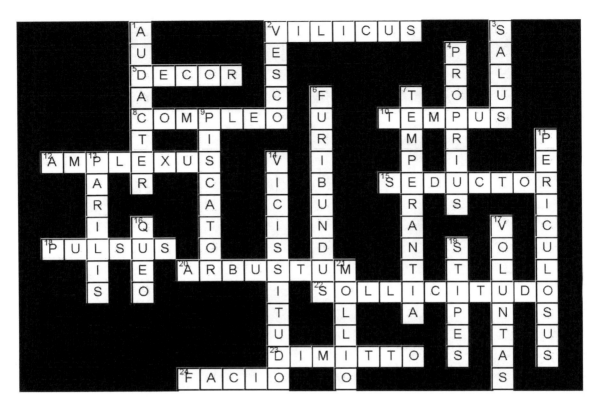

Across

2. pertaining to an estate, overseer, steward. [VILICUS]
5. beauty, grace. [DECOR]
8. to finish. [COMPLEO]
10. time. [TEMPUS]
12. an embracing, surrounding, loving embrace, [AMPLEXUS]
15. seducer. [SEDUCTOR]
18. beating, blow, push, impulse, influence. [PULSUS]
20. a vineyard planted with trees. [ARBUSTUM]
22. uneasiness, anxiety, disquiet, apprehension. [SOLLICITUDO]
23. to break up, dismiss, leave, abandon. [DIMITTO]
24. to sacrifice, suit, help, be of service. [FACIO]

Down

1. boldly, proudly, fearlessly. [AUDACTER]
2. to feed, to eat. [VESCO]
3. health, safety, well-being, salvation. [SALUS]
4. one's own, special, characteristic, particular. [PROPRIUS]
6. raging, furious. [FURIBUNDUS]
7. moderation, self-control, temperance. [TEMPERANTIA]
9. fisherman. [PISCATOR]
11. hazardous, dangerous. [PERICULOSUS]
13. similar, like, equal. [PARILIS]
14. change, alteration. [VICISSITUDO]
16. to be able. [QUEO]
17. last will, testament. [VOLUNTAS]
19. log, stump, tree trunk, branch, post, club. [STIPES]
21. to soften, make pliant. [MOLLIO]

Latin - 17

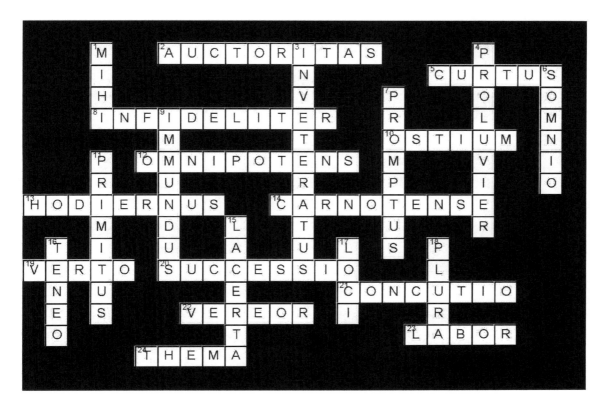

Across

2. authority [AUCTORITAS]
5. shortened; mutilated, defective; gelded. [CURTUS]
8. faithlessly, disloyally. [INFIDELITER]
10. entrance, door. [OSTIUM]
12. all-powerful, almighty, omnipotent [OMNIPOTENS]
13. of today. [HODIERNUS]
14. chartres. [CARNOTENSE]
19. to flee; interpret, understand; upset, overthrow. [VERTO]
20. succeeding, succession, descent, descendant. [SUCCESSIO]
21. to shake, disturb, agitate. [CONCUTIO]
22. to respect, fear, be in dread of, to be afraid. [VEREOR]
23. to slip, glide, slide. [LABOR]
24. theme. [THEMA]

Down

1. me [MIHI]
3. hardened by age, of long-standing. [INVETERATUS]
4. inundation; scouring; discharge. [PROLUVIER]
6. to dream; to dream of, imagine foolishly. [SOMNIO]
7. prepared, resolute, prompt. [PROMPTUS]
9. foul, impure. [IMMUNDUS]
11. first, for the first time. [PRIMITUS]
15. lizard. [LACERTA]
16. to keep on, persist, persevere, endure. [TENEO]
17. passages in literary works. [LOCI]
18. more numerous, several, many. [PLURA]

Latin - 18

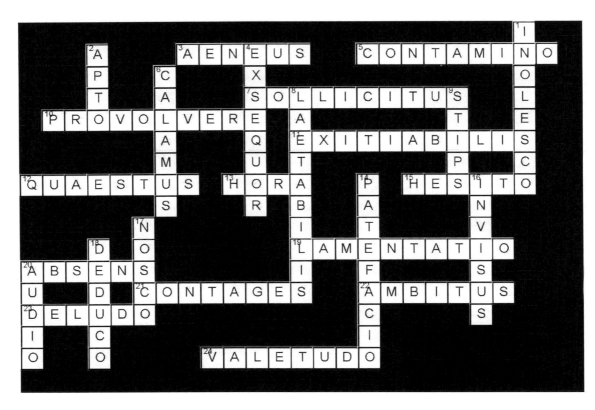

Across

3. made of copper or bronze, brazen. [AENEUS]
5. to pollute, infect. [CONTAMINO]
7. troubled, anxious, concerned, worried. [SOLLICITUS]
10. to throw oneself down, abase oneself. [PROVOLVERE]
11. fatal deadly, destructive, lethal. [EXITIABILIS]
12. profit, a source of profit, gaining, getting. [QUAESTUS]
13. hour, time. [HORA]
15. to be unsure, uncertain, wavering. [HESITO]
19. weeping, wailing, lamenting. [LAMENTATIO]
20. absent, missing, away, gone. [ABSENS]
21. a touch, contact. [CONTAGES]
22. border, edge, extent; going around, circuit. [AMBITUS]
23. to mock, cheat. [DELUDO]
24. health. good health, bad health. [VALETUDO]

Down

1. to grow in or on. [INOLESCO]
2. to fit, adapt, adjust, make ready, or fit. [APTO]
4. to maintain, keep up, carry out, fulfill, accomplish. [EXSEQUOR]
6. anything made or reed -- pen, arrow, pipe, etc. [CALAMUS]
8. joyous, glad. [LAETABILIS]
9. small coin, gift. [STIPS]
14. to disclose, expose, open, make open. [PATEFACIO]
16. hated, hateful. [INVISUS]
17. to become acquainted with, get to know. [NOSCO]
18. to lad out colonists, found a colony. [DEDUCO]
20. to hear, hearken, listen to. [AUDIO]

Latin - 19

Across

2. family, household. [FAMILIA]
4. to flee, retreat, run away. [TERGA]
6. to fish out, find out, discover. [EXPISCOR]
10. faithful, loyal, true [FIDELIS]
11. forty. [QUADRAGINTA]
13. war. [BELLUM]
14. down from, from, concerning, about. [DE]
15. nevertheless. [NICHILOMINUS]
18. air, atmosphere, ether, weather. [AER]
19. stiffness, hardness, sternness. [RIGOR]
21. to choose, prefer. [MALO]
22. claim, arrogate, assume, appropriate. [VINDICO]
23. to study, pursue eagerly, be eager for. [STUDIO]
24. theologian. [THEOLOGUS]

Down

1. theater. [THEATRUM]
3. a sharp point, edge, dagger point. [MUCRO]
5. to look back, provide for, respect, have regard for. [RESPICIO]
7. a slipping or sliding. [PROLAPSIO]
8. language, tongue, speech. [LINGUA]
9. to establish, cause, occasion. [INDO]
11. wherefore. [QUAPROPTER]
12. to keep from, refrain from. [TEMPERO]
16. : a thrower, javelin man, spear thrower. [IACULATOR]
17. second. [SECUNDUS]
20. to love, like, be fond of, cherish. [AMO]

Latin - 20

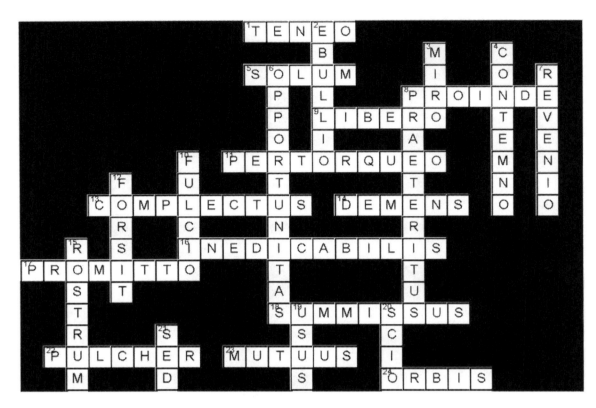

Across

1. to hold, keep, possess, maintain. [TENEO]
5. non solum ... sed etiam : not only ... but also. [SOLUM]
8. just as if. [PROINDE]
9. to lift, raise. [LIBERO]
11. to twist, distort. [PERTORQUEO]
13. embrace, grasp. [COMPLECTUS]
14. insane, mad, out of one's mind, foolish. [DEMENS]
16. unexplainable, inexplicable. [INEDICABILIS]
17. to let go forward, send forth, promise, undertake. [PROMITTO]
18. let down, lowered, gentle, mild. [SUMMISSUS]
22. beautiful, handsome, fine. [PULCHER]
23. a loan. [MUTUUS]
24. the world, the earth. [ORBIS]

Down

2. to boil up, bubble up, to appear, produce in abundance. [EBULLIO]
3. to wonder. [MIRO]
4. to think meanly of, despise, condemn, hate. [CONTEMNO]
6. fitness, suitability, convenience, advantage. [OPPORTUNITAS]
7. to come back, return. [REVENIO]
8. past. [PRAETERITUS]
10. to support, strengthen, uphold; to besiege, oppress. [FULCIO]
12. perhaps, probably. [FORSIT]
15. bill of a bird, beak. [ROSTRUM]
19. use, experience, skill, advantage. [USUS]
20. to know. [SCIO]
21. but; and indeed, what is more. [SED]

Latin - 21

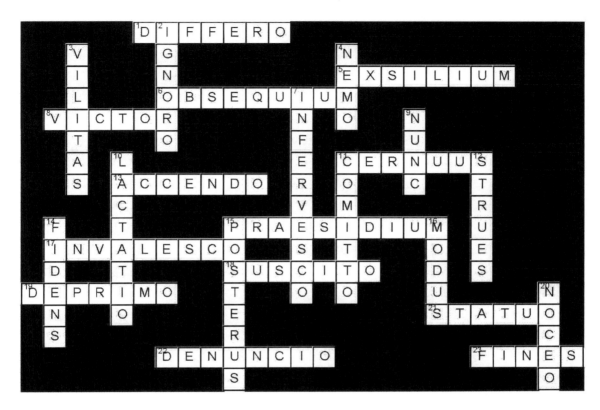

Across

1. to delay, postpone; to differ, be different. [DIFFERO]
5. exile, banishment. [EXSILIUM]
6. indulgence, pliancy, submission. [OBSEQUIUM]
8. victor, winner. [VICTOR]
11. falling headlong. [CERNUUS]
13. to kindle, illuminate, inflame. [ACCENDO]
15. guard, garrison, detachment; protection. [PRAESIDIUM]
17. to gather strength, become stronger. [INVALESCO]
18. to stir up, arouse, excite. [SUSCITO]
19. to press down, depress, low-lying. [DEPRIMO]
21. to give a ruling, make an arrangement, decide. [STATUO]
22. declare, give notice, announce. [DENUNCIO]
23. boundaries, limits,; territory. [FINES]

Down

2. to be ignorant of, not know; rarely: neglect, overlook. [IGNORO]
3. cheapness, low-price, worthlessness. [VILITAS]
4. no one, nobody. [NEMO]
7. to come to a boil, become hot. [INFERVESCO]
9. now, at the present time. [NUNC]
10. enticement, come-on. [LACTATIO]
11. to entrust, commit. [COMITTO]
12. piles, heaps, masses. [STRUES]
14. confident, without fear, courageous. [FIDENS]
15. subsequent, following, next, future. [POSTERUS]
16. measure, bound, limit; manner, method, mode, way. [MODUS]
20. to do harm to, inflict injury, hurt. [NOCEO]

Latin - 22

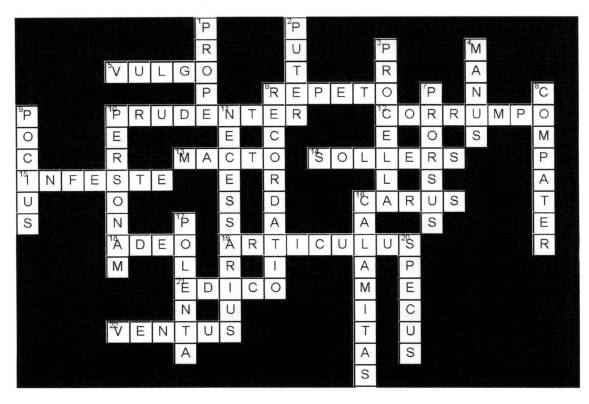

Across

5. to spread, publish, impart, make accessible. [VULGO]
6. to seek again, ask back. [REPETO]
10. wisely, discreetly. [PRUDENTER]
12. to break up, destroy, annihilate; spoil, weaken. [CORRUMPO]
13. to magnify, glorify, honor; slay, fight, punish, afflict. [MACTO]
14. clever, skillful. [SOLLERS]
15. in a hostile manner, belligerently. [INFESTE]
16. dear, beloved; costly, high-priced, expensive. [CARUS]
18. to approach, visit, come to, undertake. [ADEO]
19. a moment, crisis. [ARTICULUS]
21. to announce, declare. [EDICO]
22. wind, rumor, favor. [VENTUS]

Down

1. near, nearly, not far from, just now, closely. [PROPE]
2. rotten, decayed, putrid; loose, crumbling; flabby. [PUTER]
3. storm, tempest, gale. [PROCELLA]
4. hand, band, handwriting. [MANUS]
6. recollection, memory, recall. [RECORDATIO]
7. forward, straight ahead, to sum up, utterly, wholly. [PRORSUS]
8. the godfather of a man's child. [COMPATER]
9. rather, preferably. [POCIUS]
10. to act a part. [PERSONAM]
11. necessary, needed, essential. [NECESSARIUS]
16. calamity, misfortune, disaster. [CALAMITAS]
17. pearl barley, barley groats. [POLENTA]
20. cave, cavern, grotto, den. [SPECUS]

Latin - 23

Across

5. to drink up, suck in. [COMBIBO]
11. log, tree-trunk, branch, post, club, blockhead. [STIPES]
13. to lay out, expand, weigh out. [IMPENDO]
15. rouen. [ROTOMAGENSE]
16. to complain excessively, whine, gripe. [QUERITOR]
19. uproar, disturbance; mob, crowd, multitude. [TURBA]
20. light, slight, trivial; beardless, bald; light-armed. [LEVIS]
21. close to, near to; just before. [IUXTA]
22. to examine, inquire, learn. [COGNOSCO]
23. to run back and forth. [CURSO]

Down

1. steady, firm, unchanging, constant, unwavering. [CONSTANS]
2. industry, diligence. [INDUSTRIA]
3. to depart, deviate, digress. [DIGREDIOR]
4. benefit, favor, service, privilege, right. [BENEFICIUM]
5. civil, civic. [CIVILIS]
6. be moderate, control oneself. [TEMPERO]
7. simple, unaffected. [SIMPLEX]
8. preferring. [MALENS]
9. crossroads, place where four roads meet. [QUADRIVIUM]
10. i say. [INQUAM]
12. casting lots, deciding by lot. [SORTITUS]
14. midday, afternoon, south. [MERIDIANUS]
17. to make bright or clear, make clear in the mind. [CLARO]
18. rank, class, order. [ORDO]

Latin - 24

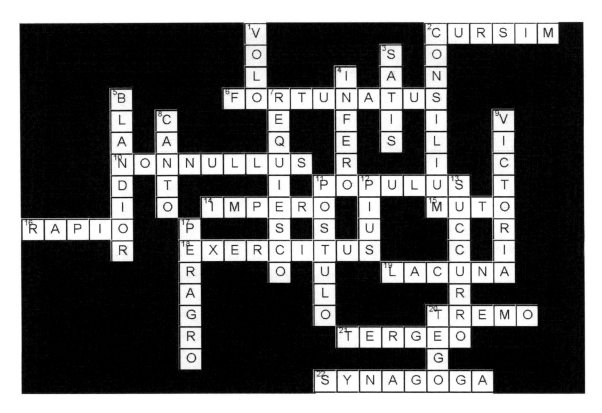

Across

2. hastily, quickly, rapidly. [CURSIM]
6. fortunate, lucky, happy. [FORTUNATUS]
10. some [NONNULLUS]
11. people, the people, nation, crowd, multitude, host. [POPULUS]
14. to give orders, command; to rule, hold sway. [IMPERO]
15. punish, fine, mulct. [MUTO]
16. to seize, snatch, carry away. [RAPIO]
18. army. [EXERCITUS]
19. missing letters, words, or phrases in a manuscript. [LACUNA]
20. to tremble, shake, shudder. [TREMO]
21. to wipe, scour, clean [TERGEO]
22. synagogue. [SYNAGOGA]

Down

1. to fly, speed, move rapidly. [VOLO]
2. deliberation, consultation, assembly, council. [CONSILIUM]
3. enough, sufficient; sufficiently. [SATIS]
4. to carry in, put or place on. [INFERO]
5. to flatter, caress, coax. [BLANDIOR]
7. to rest. [REQUIESCO]
8. to sing. [CANTO]
9. victory. [VICTORIA]
11. to ask. [POSTULO]
12. dutiful, godly, holy, upright, kind, honest, affectionate. [PIUS]
13. to run up under; aid, assist, help. [SUCCURRO]
17. to wander through, travel through. [PERAGRO]
20. to cover, bury, conceal, hide, protect, shield. [TEGO]

Latin - 25

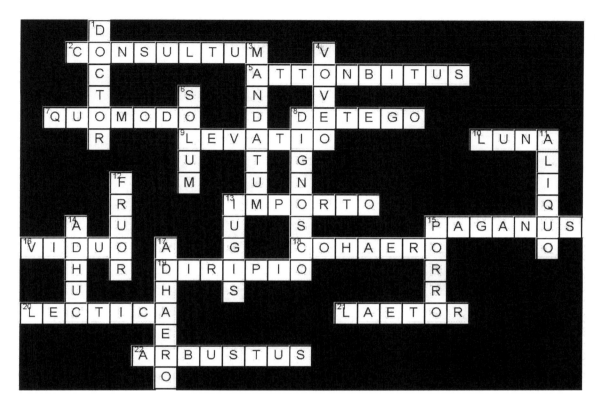

Across

2. decree. [CONSULTUM]
5. frantic, inspired, thunder-struck, stunned. [ATTONBITUS]
7. in what manner, how; in whatever way, somehow. [QUOMODO]
8. to uncover, lay bare, disclose. [DETEGO]
9. alleviation, mitigation, solace. [LEVATIO]
10. moon. [LUNA]
13. to bring in, introduce, import; bring upon, cause. [IMPORTO]
15. countryman, peasant, pagan. [PAGANUS]
16. to deprive [VIDUO]
18. to adhere, stick together [COHAERO]
19. to separate, tear apart; pillage, devastate, lay waste. [DIRIPIO]
20. litter, bier. [LECTICA]
21. to rejoice, be joyful. [LAETOR]
22. planted with trees. [ARBUSTUS]

Down

1. teacher. [DOCTOR]
3. order, decree, mandate, instruction. [MANDATUM]
4. to promise to god, vow, pray for. [VOVEO]
6. land, country, soil, ground; bottom, floor, foundation. [SOLUM]
8. to distinguish, recognize as different. [DIGNOSCO]
11. in some direction. [ALIQUO]
12. to have the benefit of, to enjoy. [FRUOR]
13. perpetual, continuous. [IUGIS]
14. till then, till now, still, even now, besides, also, yet. [ADHUC]
15. forward, further, next, in turn. [PORRO]
17. to hang to, stick to, adhere. [ADHAERO]

Latin - 26

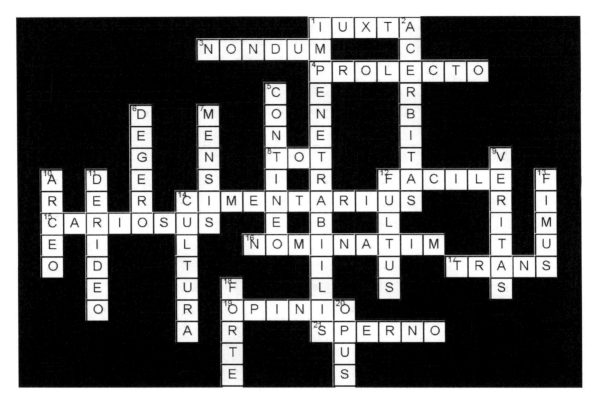

Across

1. just short of. [IUXTA]
3. not yet [NONDUM]
4. to entice, allure. [PROLECTO]
8. so many. [TOT]
12. easily. [FACILE]
14. mason [CIMENTARIUS]
15. rotten, decayed. [CARIOSUS]
16. by name, expressly. [NOMINATIM]
17. across. [TRANS]
19. opinion, report, rumor, conjecture, report. [OPINIO]
21. to scorn, despise, spurn. [SPERNO]

Down

1. impenetrable. [IMPENETRABIILIS]
2. harshness, bitterness. [ACERBITAS]
5. to keep in, surround, contain, confine, include. [CONTINEO]
6. to pass time, live. [DEGERO]
7. month. [MENSIS]
9. truth. [VERITAS]
10. to shut up, enclose. [ARCEO]
11. to laugh at, mock, deride. [DERIDEO]
12. supporter. [FULTUS]
13. dung, dirt, filth, manure. [FIMUS]
14. cultivation [CULTURA]
18. by chance, by luck, accidentally. [FORTE]
20. work, labor, work done, completed work, building. [OPUS]

Latin - 27

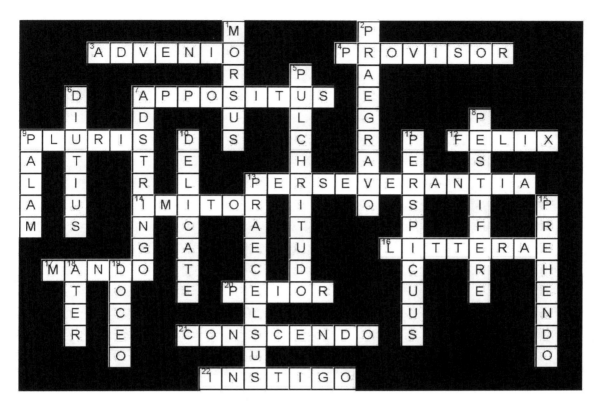

Across

3. to come, arrive, reach. [ADVENIO]
4. one who provides for, or against. [PROVISOR]
7. placed near, approaching, appropriate, appositively. [APPOSITUS]
9. at a higher price, of a great value [PLURIS]
12. lucky, fortunate, happy. [FELIX]
13. perseverance, persistence. [PERSEVERANTIA]

14. to imitate. [IMITOR]
16. letter, epistle, missive, note; literature. [LITTERAE]
17. to commit, entrust, order, command. [MANDO]
20. worse. [PEIOR]
21. to ascend, mount, go up. [CONSCENDO]
22. to goad, incite, stimulate, urge. [INSTIGO]

Down

1. a biting, bite, also, sting, pain. [MORSUS]
2. to press heavily upon, weigh down, oppress. [PRAEGRAVO]
5. beauty, fineness. [PULCHRITUDO]
6. longer, too long. [DIUTIUS]
7. to draw together, tighten, bind. [ADSTRINGO]
8. destructively, injuriously. [PESTIFERE]
9. openly, publicly, in the presence of. [PALAM]
10. luxuriously. [DELICATE]
11. transparent, bright, clear, evident. [PERSPICUUS]
13. exceedingly high. [PRAECELSUS]
15. to seize, snatch, grasp, detain, arrest. [PREHENDO]
18. dark. [ATER]
19. to instruct, teach, tutor. [DOCEO]

Latin - 28

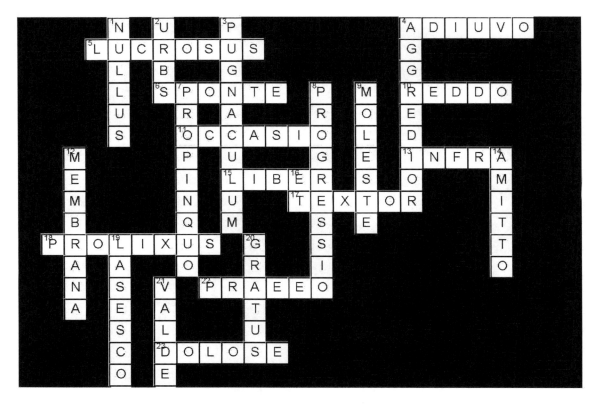

Across

4. to help, aid, assist. [ADIUVO]
5. profitable, gainful. [LUCROSUS]
6. willingly, of one's own accord, unaided. [SPONTE]
10. to repeat, recite, represent, imitate, pay up, deliver. [REDDO]
11. favorable moment, opportunity. [OCCASIO]
13. low down. [INFRA]
15. child, offspring. [LIBER]
17. weaver. [TEXTOR]
18. wide, broad, long; willing, obliging, favorable. [PROLIXUS]
22. to go before, precede; to say in advance. [PRAEEO]
23. slyly, deceitfully. [DOLOSE]

Down

1. not any, no, none. [NULLUS]
2. city. [URBS]
3. fortress. [PUGNACULUM]
4. to go to, approach, address, attack. [AGGREDIOR]
7. to come near, draw near, approach. [PROPINQUO]
8. advance, progress, increase. [PROGRESSIO]
9. take annoyance [MOLESTE]
12. thin skin, film, parchment, membrane, prepared skin. [MEMBRANA]
14. to send away, let go, let slip, lose. [AMITTO]
16. both ... and. [ET]
19. to become tired, grow weary. [LASESCO]
20. pleasing, agreeable; grateful. [GRATUS]
21. intensely, very much, extremely, greatly [VALDE]

Latin - 29

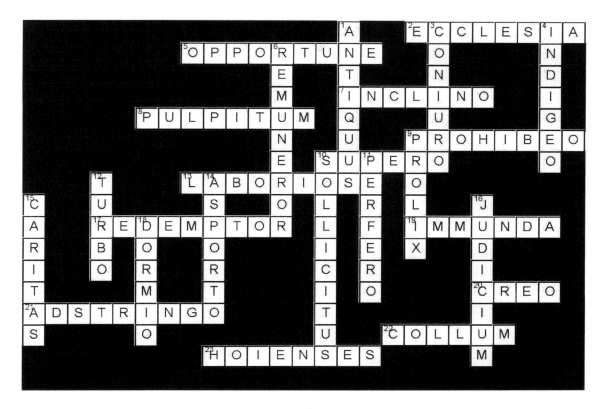

Across

2. church. [ECCLESIA]
5. opportunely, conveniently. [OPPORTUNE]
7. to bend, incline, turn, change; fall back, waver. [INCLINO]
8. platform, stage. [PULPITUM]
9. to prevent, hinder, restrain, prohibit, forbid. [PROHIBEO]
10. to be above, have the upper hand, surpass, conquer, overcome. [SUPERO]
13. laboriously, with great effort [LABORIOSE]
17. redeemer. [REDEMPTOR]
19. unclean, impure, dirty, foul. [IMMUNDA]
20. to create, make. [CREO]
21. bind, oblige,. [ADSTRINGO]
22. neck. [COLLUM]
23. huy, belgium, between liege and namur. [HOIENSES]

Down

1. ancient, old, hoary, [ANTIQUUS]
3. to take an oath together, plot, conspire. [CONIURO]
4. to require, need, stand in need of. [INDIGEO]
6. to repay, reward. [REMUNEROR]
9. long, stretching. [PROLIX]
10. uneasy, worried, anxious, restless, agitated. [SOLLICITUS]
11. to bear, suffer, endure. [PERFERO]
12. to disturb, upset, throw into disorder, confuse, unsettle. [TURBO]
14. to carry off, take away. [ASPORTO]
15. dearness, affection; charity. [CARITAS]
16. trial, legal investigation, judgement, decision. [JUDICIUM]
18. to sleep, slumber, siesta, nap. [DORMIO]

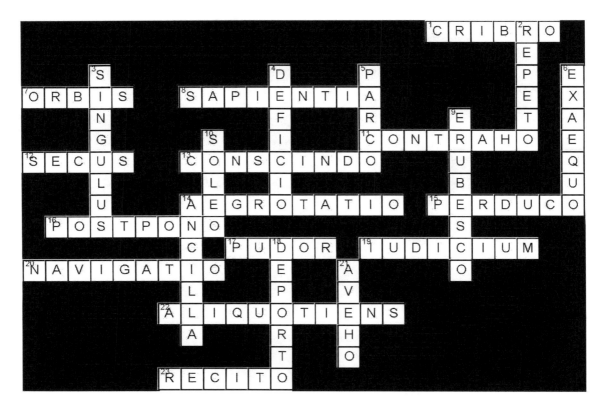

Across

1. to sift. [CRIBRO]
7. circle, orb. [ORBIS]
8. wisdom. [SAPIENTIA]
11. to draw together, collect, assemble, carry out. [CONTRAHO]
12. otherwise, not so. [SECUS]
13. to tear in pieces. [CONSCINDO]
14. sickness, illness. [AEGROTATIO]
15. to lead through, conduct, carry through. [PERDUCO]
16. to put after, consider secondary. [POSTPONO]
17. modesty, bashfulness. [PUDOR]
19. judgment, decision, opinion, trial [IUDICIUM]
20. voyage, navigation. [NAVIGATIO]
22. some times. [ALIQUOTIENS]
23. to read aloud, recite. [RECITO]

Down

2. to return to, begin again, deduce, recall, recollect. [REPETO]
3. single, separate, one at a time, one each. [SINGULUS]
4. to fail, to weaken, to be in want. [DEFICIO]
5. to spare, refrain from injuring. [PARCO]
6. to be like, equal; make level or even, relate. [EXAEQUO]
9. to blush, grow red, be ashamed. [ERUBESCO]
10. to be accustomed, be used to. [SOLEO]
14. maidservant, also used by nuns to describe themselves. [ANCILLA]
18. to carry off, to take away. [DEPORTO]
21. to carry away, remove. [AVEHO]

Latin - 31

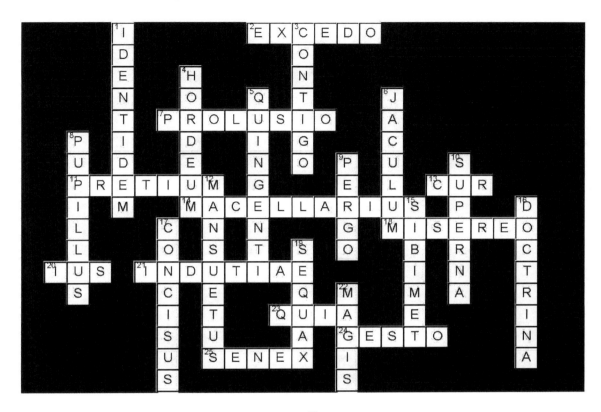

Across

2. to exceed, leave, pass beyond. [EXCEDO]
7. preliminary exercise, prelude. [PROLUSIO]
11. price, value, reward. [PRETIUM]
13. why, wherefore. [CUR]
14. butcher, slaughter-house. [MACELLARIUS]
18. to pity. [MISEREO]
20. oath. [IUS]
21. truce, armistice, suspension of hostilities. [INDUTIAE]
23. because. [QUIA]
24. to carry, bear about. [GESTO]
25. old, aged, old man. [SENEX]

Down

1. again and again, repeatedly. [IDENTIDEM]
3. to happen, befall. [CONTIGO]
4. barley. [HORDEUM]
5. five hundred. [QUINGENTI]
6. dart, javelin. [JACULUM]
8. orphan, ward. [PUPILLUS]
9. to continue, proceed, go on with. [PERGO]
10. northeast by north wind. [SUPERNA]
12. mild, soft, gentle. [MANSUETUS]
15. to them themselves. [SIBIMET]
16. doctrine, teaching, instruction, learning. [DOCTRINA]
17. cut up, broken, brief, concise. [CONCISUS]
19. following, attending, pursuing. [SEQUAX]
22. more, to a greater extent, rather, for preference [MAGIS]

Latin - 32

Across

3. servant. [FAMULUS]
4. today. [HODIE]
5. to take one's stand, stand still, stop, be posted. [CONSISTO]
6. partly; some. [PARTIM]
8. sound, healthy, sane. [SANUS]
9. modest. chaste. [PUDICUS]
12. to obtain, get, acquire. [ADEPTO]
14. chiefly, especially, particularly. [PRECIPUE]
17. avenging, punishment, revenge. [ULTIO]
18. to be seen, seem, appear. [VIDEOR]
21. cold, coolness, cold of winter; dullness, indolence. [FRIGUS]
22. commander in chief, general, emperor. [IMPERATOR]
23. to set in mortion, impel, urge on. [IMPELLO]

Down

1. eagerly, earnestly. [CONTENTE]
2. customary, usual. [USITAS]
3. fortune, luck, fate, chance. [FORTUNA]
7. honey. [MEL]
8. humbly, softly, calmly, modestly. [SUMMISSE]
10. to intercept [INTERCIPIO]
11. porter, pall-bearer, carrier of a burden. [BAIULUS]
13. judgment, case; plea, litigation; defense. [PLACITUM]
15. mother. [MATER]
16. nothingness, worthlessness, vanity. [IRRITUM]
19. thing, matter, business, affair. [RES]
20. to lead, induce, persuade. [ADDUCO]

Latin - 33

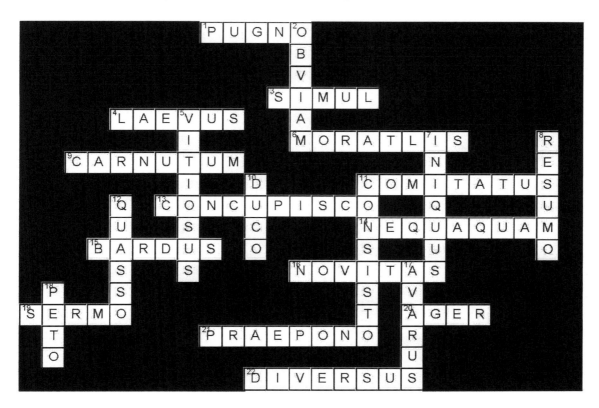

Across

1. to fight. [PUGNO]
3. as soon as. [SIMUL]
4. the left hand, left side, left-handed. [LAEVUS]
6. mortal. [MORATLIS]
9. chartres. [CARNUTUM]
11. train, retinue [COMITATUS]
13. to covet, aim at, desire eagerly. [CONCUPISCO]
14. by no means, not at all. [NEQUAQUAM]
15. stupid, slow, dull. [BARDUS]
16. newness, novelty, strangeness. [NOVITAS]
19. talk, common talk, rumor [SERMO]
20. farm, field, acre. [AGER]
21. to set over, prefer. [PRAEPONO]
22. different, unlike, opposed, hostile. [DIVERSUS]

Down

2. on the way, in the way; towards, against. [OBVIAM]
5. vicious, full of vice, corrupt. [VITIOSUS]
7. unequal, unjust, unfair. [INIQUUS]
8. to renew, repeat, resume. [RESUMO]
10. to charm, influence, mislead, draw in. [DUCO]
11. to depend on, rely on. [CONSISTO]
12. to shake violently, shake to pieces, break, shatter.. [QUASSO]
17. greedy, avaricious. [AVARUS]
18. to make for, go to, seek, strive after. [PETO]

Latin - 34

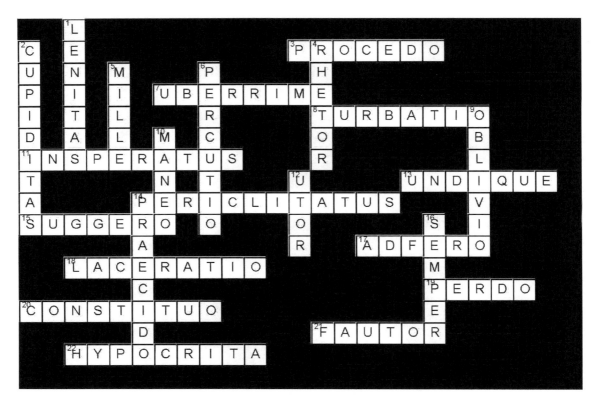

Across

3. to go out, come out. [PROCEDO]
7. most luxuriantly, most abundantly [UBERRIME]
8. disturbance, confusion. [TURBATIO]
11. unexpected, unlooked for, unanticipated. [INSPERATUS]
13. from all sides, everywhere [UNDIQUE]
14. put in peril, endangered. [PERICLITATUS]
15. to bring up, supply, provide, add [SUGGERO]
17. to bring news, report. [ADFERO]
18. a tearing, mangling. [LACERATIO]
19. to destroy, ruin, waste, scatter, squander. [PERDO]
20. to set up, place [CONSTITUO]
21. favorer, promoter, patron, partisan, supporter. [FAUTOR]
22. hypocrite [HYPOCRITA]

Down

1. smoothness, gentleness, mildness. [LENITAS]
2. ambition, avarice [CUPIDITAS]
4. rhetorician, teacher of rhetoric. [RHETOR]
5. a thousand. [MILLE]
6. to strike hard, pierce [PERCUTIO]
9. forgetfulness, oblivion. [OBLIVIO]
10. to remain, stay, stay the night [MANEO]
12. to use, employ, possess, enjoy. [UTOR]
14. to cut short, lop, mutilate. [PRAECIDO]
16. always, ever. [SEMPER]

Across

1. indiscriminately. [PROMISCE]
2. school; elite troop of soldiers. [SCHOLA]
5. combined in one, whole, entire. [UNIVERSUS]
7. to be strong, have power, be well. [VALEO]
10. to remember, recollect. [COMMONEO]
12. to set free, deliver, liberate, release; exempt [LIBERO]
13. to be unlike one's kind, fall off, degenerate. [DEGENERO]
14. silver, money. [ARGENTUM]
16. countess. [COMETISSA]
18. case, envelope, covering. [THECA]
20. to care for, trouble about, pay attention to. [CURO]
22. quickly, rapidly, speedily. [CITO]
23. to play the fool, to trifle. [INEPTIO]
24. of any kind whatever, any whatever. [QUALISCUMQUE]

Down

1. beggardry, poverty, humble circumstances. [PAUPERTAS]
3. shave, shear, clip, mow, reap, browse. [TONDEO]
4. to chide, rebuke. [INCREPO]
6. to struggle against, resist. [RELUCTOR]
8. weeping, wailing. [LAMENTA]
9. partner, comrade, associate, ally, fellow. [SOCIUS]
11. to cool, grow lukewarm, decrease. [TEPESCO]
15. by the roots, utterly. [RADICITUS]
17. bending, curving. [INFLEXUS]
19. cross. [CRUX]
21. deed, accomplishment, work, act, achievement. [FACTUM]

Latin - 36

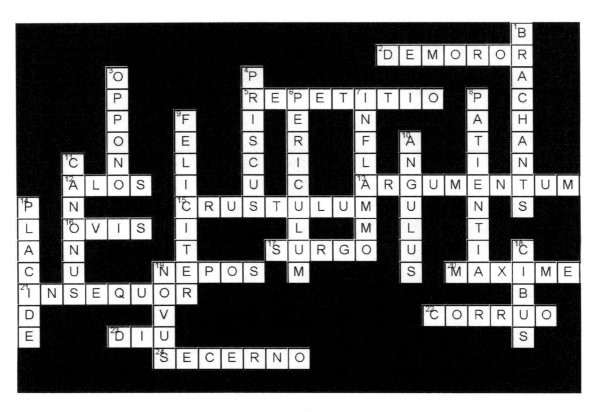

Across

2. to loiter, linger, tarry, belay. [DEMOROR]
5. repetition. [REPETITIO]
12. alquod: some. [ALOS]
13. proof, evidence. [ARGUMENTUM]
15. pastry, cookie. [CRUSTULUM]
16. sheep. [OVIS]
17. to get up arise. [SURGO]
19. grandson. [NEPOS]
20. especially, particularly, principally. [MAXIME]
21. to follow, pursue, assail, reproach, rebuke, attack. [INSEQUOR]
22. to fall to the ground, sink down; be ruined, destroyed. [CORRUO]
23. adv. a long while, long time, for a long time. [DIU]
24. to separate. [SECERNO]

Down

1. brabant. [BRACHANTS]
3. to set against, oppose, be opposite. [OPPONO]
4. ancient, antique, former, old days, venerable. [PRISCUS]
6. danger, risk. [PERICULUM]
7. to set on fire, inflame, to torch, kindle. [INFLAMMO]
8. patience, suffering, endurance. [PATIENTIA]
9. happily. [FELICITER]
10. corner, niche. [ANGULUS]
11. canon, member of a cathedral chapter or canonry, augustinian. [CANONUS]
14. quitely, gently. [PLACIDE]
18. food for men and animals. [CIBUS]
19. novel, unusual, extraordinary; news, novelty, a new thing [NOVUS]

Latin - 37

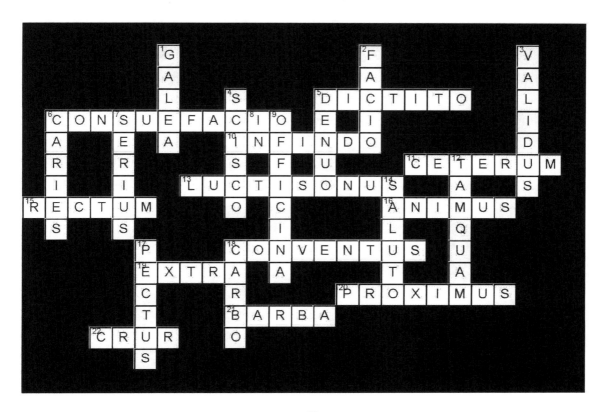

Across

5. to say often, reiterate. [DICTITO]
6. to accustom, acclimate, become used to. [CONSUEFACIO]
10. to cut into. [INFINDO]
11. otherwise, moreover, but. [CETERUM]
13. sad-sounding, mournful, baleful. [LUCTISONUS]
15. virtue, right [RECTUM]
16. character, intellect, memory, consciousness, often mind. [ANIMUS]
18. coming together, assembly, union, congress. [CONVENTUS]
19. beyond, outside. [EXTRA]
20. nearest, closest, next. [PROXIMUS]
21. beard, whiskers. [BARBA]
22. leg, shank, shin, also foot. [CRUR]

Down

1. helmet. [GALEA]
2. to give permission; to experience, suffer. [FACIO]
3. strong, mighty, powerful, exceeding. [VALIDUS]
4. investigate, ask, inquire; vote, ordain, resolve. [SCISCO]
5. anew, again, a second time, afresh. [DENUO]
6. rottenness, corruption, decay. [CARIES]
7. serious, grave, solemn. [SERIUS]
8. into, toward, against. [IN]
9. workshop, factor. [OFFICINA]
12. as, just as, like as, just as if. [TAMQUAM]
14. to wish well, greet, visit, reverence, pay respect to. [SALUTO]
17. heart, breast. [PECTUS]
18. carbon, coal, charcoal. [CARBO]

Latin - 38

Across

1. uncommonness, excellence. [EXIMIETATE]
6. to be angry, to be wrathful. [IRASCOR]
8. creature, servant. [CREATURA]
9. to praise, extoll, commend; name, mention, cite, quote. [LAUDO]
12. quiet, still, gentle. [PLACIDUS]
14. fugitive : deserter, runaway slave. [FUGITIVUS]
15. firm, resolved, staunch. [OBSTINATUS]
16. agreement, contract, covenant, pact. [PACTUM]
17. wandering, vagrant, itinerant. [VULGIVAGUS]
21. within. [INTUS]
22. to carry out, bring forth. [PROFERO]
23. careful, attentive; curious, inquisitive; worn out by cares. [CURIOSUS]

Down

2. triumphal procession, triumph. [TRIUMPHUS]
3. to give a nod to, give a sign to. [INNUO]
4. a thousand times. [MILLIES]
5. talk, report, rumor, tradition. [FAMA]
7. to refuse. [RECUSO]
10. put before, prefer, favor, promote. [ANTEPONO]
11. get the start of. [PRAEVENIO]
12. to carry on, carry forward, advance, promote, [PROVEHO]
13. those down below, the dead. [INFERI]
14. to occupy oneself, perform, do, execute. [FUNGOR]
18. gain, profit. [LUCRUM]
19. pure, free from. [PURUS]
20. to destroy, wipe out, erase. [DELEO]

Latin - 39

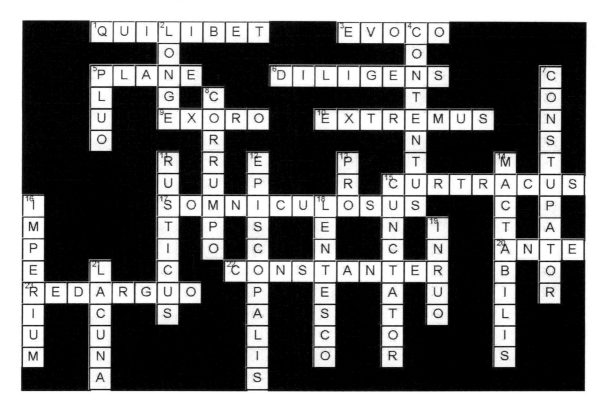

Across

1. anyone, anything. [QUILIBET]
3. to draw out, draw on, produce, recall to the colors. [EVOCO]
5. plainly, clearly. [PLANE]
6. diligent, careful. [DILIGENS]
9. to prevail upon a person, entreat successfully. [EXORO]
10. outermost, last, extreme. [EXTREMUS]
15. courtrai. [CURTRACUS]
17. sleepy, drowsy [SOMNICULOSUS]
20. before; in front of; before, previously. [ANTE]
22. steadily, firmly. [CONSTANTER]
23. refute, disprove, contradict. [REDARGUO]

Down

2. far. [LONGE]
4. strained, stretched; eager, zealous. [CONTENTUS]
5. to rain, shower, sprinkle. [PLUO]
7. ravisher, debaucher. [CONSTUPATOR]
8. to falsify; to corrupt. [CORRUMPO]
11. rustic, rural; peasant. [RUSTICUS]
12. episcopal [EPISCOPALIS]
13. in return for, instead of; for, as. [PRO]
14. deadly, lethal. [MACTABILIS]
15. delayer, procrastinator, [CUNCTATOR]
16. power to command, authority, command, rule, control. [IMPERIUM]
18. to become soft, flexible, sticky; to weaken, slacken. [LENTESCO]
19. to rush in, fling in. [INRUO]
21. a hole, empty space; pond, pool; deficiency, loss. [LACUNA]

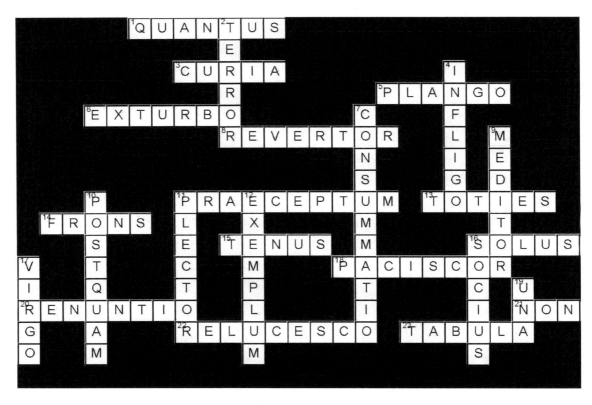

Across

1. how great? [QUANTUS]
3. court [CURIA]
5. to strike, beat; bewail, mourn. [PLANGO]
6. to drive away, thrust out. [EXTURBO]
8. to return, come back. [REVERTOR]
11. precept. [PRAECEPTUM]
13. so often, so many times. [TOTIES]
14. forehead, brow, front. [FRONS]
15. up to, down to as far as. [TENUS]
16. alone, only, the only. [SOLUS]
18. to make a bargain or agreement, covenant, deal. [PACISCOR]
20. to declare, announce, report, give notice. [RENUNTIO]
21. not. [NON]
22. to become bright again. [RELUCESCO]
23. board, plank, gaming board, painted panel. [TABULA]

Down

2. fright, fear, terror. [TERROR]
4. to strike, hit, knock; cause damage. [INFLIGO]
7. completion, summing up, adding up. [CONSUMMATIO]
9. to reflect upon, consider, ponder; practice. [MEDITOR]
10. after. [POSTQUAM]
11. to be punished. [PLECTOR]
12. pattern, model, example . [EXEMPLUM]
16. sharing, associated, allied. [SOCIUS]
17. maiden, virgin, young girl. [VIRGO]
19. in one, together. [UNA]

Latin - 41

Across

3. corbie. [CORBEIAM]
6. knowledge, science, skill. [SCIENTIA]
9. undecided, void, unfixed, of no effect. [IRRITUS]

10. thorough, tense, anxious, strict. [INTENTUS]
11. worry, fatigue, vex, harass, tease. [FATIGO]
13. wetness, moisture. [MADOR]
15. to wander, stray, rove; be mistaken, err, go astray. [ERRO]
17. to shorten, abbreviate. [CURTO]
18. new, fresh, young, inexperienced, revived, refreshed. [NOVUS]
19. wicked, accursed, infamous, criminal. [SCELERATUS]
20. stuffed full, crammed, jammed. [DIFFERTUS]
21. feeling, sense. [SENSUS]

Down

1. to chirp, tweet, pipe. [PIPIO]
2. to act foolishly, play the fool, make an ass of one's self. [DESIPIO]
4. to implore, entreat, beg, call as a witness. [OBTESTOR]
5. beautiful, pretty, charming, handsome. [BELLUS]
7. notice sent to a higher tribunal. [APOSTOLUS]
8. to hasten; accelerate, speed up. [PROPERO]
12. ground, earth, soil; land, country. [HUMUS]
14. ninth. [NONUS]
15. even, also. [ETIAM]
16. sword. [GLADIUS]
17. all, all collectively, the whole. [CUNCTUS]

Latin - 42

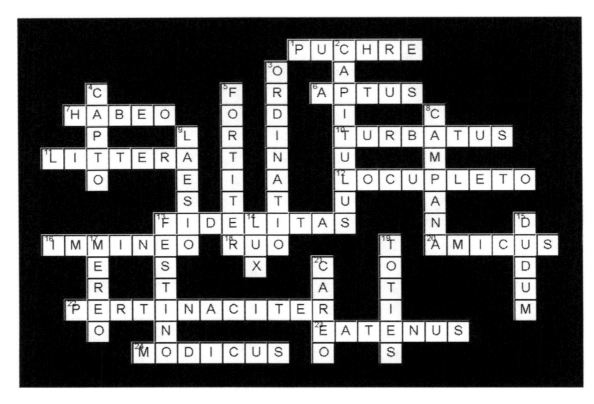

Across

1. beautifully, finely, handsomely. [PUCHRE]
6. fitted, connected, fastened; prepared, fitted out. [APTUS]
7. to have, hold, possess; consider, regard. [HABEO]
10. angered, exasperated; disturbed, restless, troubled. [TURBATUS]
11. letter. [LITTERA]
12. to enrich, make wealthy. [LOCUPLETO]
13. fidelity, loyalty, homage. [FIDELITAS]
16. to hang over, be imminent, threaten. [IMMINEO]
18. to rush, fall, be ruined. [RUO]
20. friend, comrade. [AMICUS]
22. stubbornly, obstinately. [PERTINACITER]
23. so far, thus far, up to then. [EATENUS]
24. ordinary, undistinguished, within bounds. [MODICUS]

Down

2. chapter, chapter meeting, chapter house. [CAPITULUS]
3. rule, government, order, arrangment, regulation. [ORDINATIO]
4. to grab, try to get, grab at. [CAPTO]
5. strongly, bravely. [FORTITER]
8. bell. [CAMPANA]
9. rhetorical attack; wounding. [LAESIO]
13. to hasten, hurry, speed. [FESTINO]
14. light. [LUX]
15. for a long while, a long while ago, some time age. [DUDUM]
17. deserve, earn, be entitled to, merit. [MEREO]
19. often, so many times. [TOTIES]
21. be without, be deprived of, lack, want. [CAREO]

Latin - 43

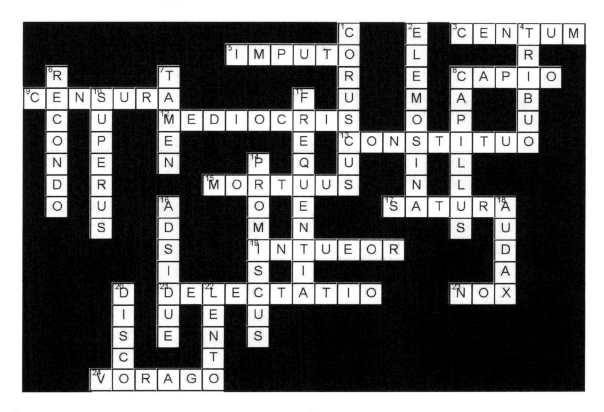

Across

3. one hundred, 100. [CENTUM]
5. to lay to a charge, enter in an account, impute to. [IMPUTO]
8. to seize, take, choose; attack, injure; comprehend. [CAPIO]
9. judgement. [CENSURA]
12. ordinary, average, fair, moderate, mediocre. [MEDIOCRIS]
13. to arrange, decide, appoint, settle, found, set up. [CONSTITUO]
15. dead, deceased, passed away, gone west, departed. [MORTUUS]
17. satire. [SATURA]
19. to look at attentively, gaze at, consider. [INTUEOR]
21. delight, pleasure, enjoyment. [DELECTATIO]
23. night. [NOX]
24. chasm, pit, abyss. [VORAGO]

Down

1. flashing, twinkling, shaking, trembling. [CORUSCUS]
2. alms [ELEMOSINA]
4. to give out, divide, allot, assign, grant, give, allow. [TRIBUO]
6. lay up, store, hoard. [RECONDO]
7. notwithstanding, nevertheless, yet, still, for all that. [TAMEN]
8. hair. [CAPILLUS]
10. above, upper, high. [SUPERUS]
11. a large concourse, population, numerous assembly. [FREQUENTIA]
14. mixed, indiscriminate; commonplace, usual. [PROMISCUS]
16. continuously, without remission. [ADSIDUE]
18. bold [AUDAX]
20. to learn, become acquainted with. [DISCO]
22. to bend. [LENTO]

Latin - 44

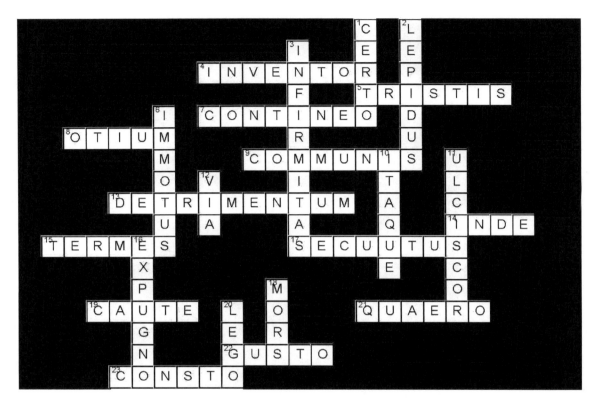

Across

4. inventor, discoverer. [INVENTOR]
5. sad, gloomy, downcast. [TRISTIS]
7. to touch, reach, grasp, affect, infect. [CONTINEO]
8. free time, leisure, ease, peace, repose. [OTIUM]
9. common, general, run of the mill. [COMMUNIS]
13. damage, loss, detriment. [DETRIMENTUM]
14. thence, from there, for that reason, thereafter, then. [INDE]
15. a tree branch. [TERMES]
17. follower, pursuer. [SECUUTUS]
19. cautiously, with security. [CAUTE]
21. to seek, search for; ask, enquire, search for [QUAERO]
22. to taste. [GUSTO]
23. to be established, stand firm, stop, endure. [CONSTO]

Down

1. to contend, settle, dispute, to settle by combat. [CERTO]
2. charming, witty, pleasant, elegant. [LEPIDUS]
3. weakness, feebleness; instability, fickleness. [INFIRMITAS]
6. unmoved. [IMMOTUS]
10. and, so, therefore. [ITAQUE]
11. to take vengeance for, avenge. [ULCISCOR]
12. road, way, street. [VIA]
16. to capture, overcome, subdue.. [EXPUGNO]
18. death. [MORS]
20. to gather, choose, collect, pass through, read, [LEGO]

Latin - 45

Across

1. have confidence in, be confident of, rely upon. [CONFIDO]
4. a dwarf. [PUMILIUS]
7. threshold. [LIMEN]
8. defense, protection [TUTAMEN]
9. agreeing, fit, suitable. [CONGRUUS]
12. to draw out, protract, defer, make known. [PROTRAHO]
13. to pick out, select, choose. [ELIGO]
14. to remain behind, stay, continue. [REMANEO]
16. thence, next; thereupon, after that, then; accordingly. [EXINDE]
17. step-daughter. [PRIVIGNA]
19. to limp, halt, be lame, to hobble. [CLAUDEO]
20. slave, serf. [SERVUS]
21. from above, above. [SUPERNE]
22. grace, indulgence, favor, pardon, forgiveness. [VENIA]

Down

1. loud shouting, cry. [CLAMOR]
2. means, wealth, abundance, riches, resources. [OPES]
3. fortifying, defense works, bridging, fortification. [MUNITIO]
5. maternal aunt. [MATERTERA]
6. to direct one's course, tend, make or head for. [TENDO]
10. firm, stable, steadfast. [STABILIS]
11. to speak, argue, plead, orate, beg, entreat. [ORO]
12. inside, widely, through and through, completely. [PENITUS]
15. magical. [MAGUS]
16. to inform fully, instruct thoroughly. [EDOCEO]
18. fame, renown, glory. [GLORIA]

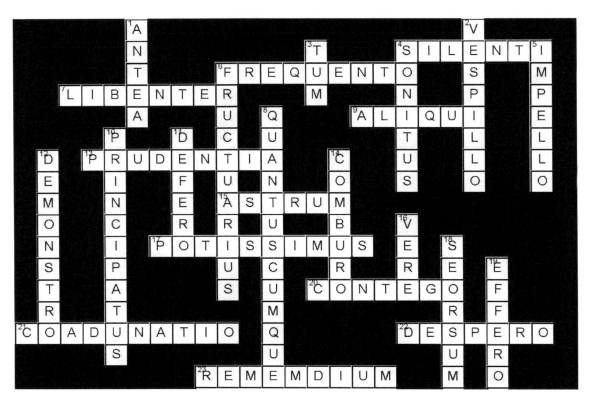

Across

4. the dead. [SILENTI]
6. to crowd, collect in large number, visit. [FREQUENTO]
7. willingly, with pleasure. [LIBENTER]
9. some. [ALIQUI]
13. foresight, wisdom, discretion. [PRUDENTIA]
15. star, constellation. [ASTRUM]
17. best of all, chief, principal. [POTISSIMUS]
20. to cover, shield, protect, defend. [CONTEGO]
21. a gathering together, a summing up, a uniting. [COADUNATIO]
22. to have no hope, despair, give up. [DESPERO]
23. cure, remedy, nostrum, medicine. [REMEMDIUM]

Down

1. before, previously, formerly. [ANTEA]
2. undertaker. [VESPILLO]
3. at that time, then; thereupon, in the next place. [TUM]
4. noise, sound. [SONITUS]
5. to drive against, strike upon. [IMPELLO]
6. fruitful, fertile. [FRUCTUARIUS]
8. however great [QUANTUSCUMQUE]
10. rule, dominion, pre-eminence, first place. [PRINCIPATUS]
11. to hand over, carry down, communicate, offer, refer. [DEFERO]
12. to indicate, show, describe, explain. [DEMONSTRO]
14. to burn up, to ruin, consume. [COMBURO]
16. truly, really, actually, rightly. [VERE]
18. apart, separately. [SEORSUM]
19. to carry out, bury, lift up, exalt. [EFFERO]

Latin - 47

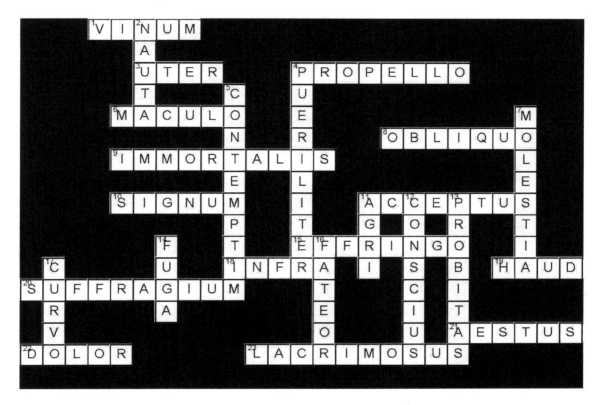

Across

1. wine. [VINUM]
3. either of the two [UTER]
4. to drive before one, drive away. [PROPELLO]
6. to stain, blemish, defile, pollute. [MACULO]
8. to turn sideways, turn aside. [OBLIQUO]
9. immortal. [IMMORTALIS]
10. sign, seal, indication, sign. [SIGNUM]
11. welcome, pleasant, agreeable. [ACCEPTUS]
15. break, break open. [EFFRINGO]
18. below, underneath; to the south, in the underworld. [INFRA]
19. no, not at all, by no means. [HAUD]
20. vote, franchise; approval support, aid, assistance. [SUFFRAGIUM]
21. heat, tide. [AESTUS]
22. pain, grief. misery, pain, suffering. [DOLOR]
23. tearful, mournful, shedding tears, [LACRIMOSUS]

Down

2. sailor. [NAUTA]
4. boyishly, childishly, foolishly. [PUERILITER]
5. contemptuously. [CONTEMPTIM]
7. annoyance, troublesomeness; stiffness, affectation. [MOLESTIA]
11. farm, field, acre. [AGRI]
12. conscious of, aware of. [CONSCIUS]
13. probity, uprightness, honesty. [PROBITAS]
14. flight, escape, [FUGA]
16. to confess, admit, allow, reveal, make known. [FATEOR]
17. to bend, arch, curve; influence. [CURVO]

Latin - 48

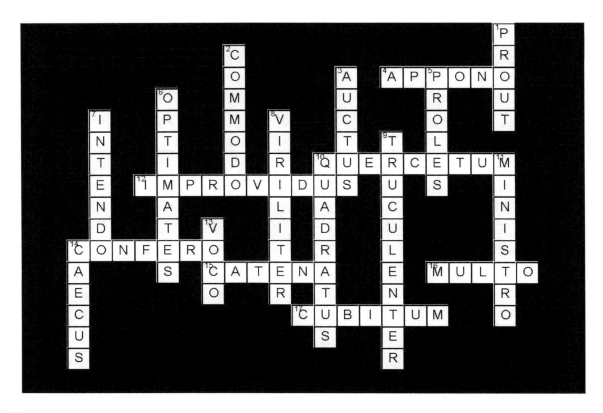

Across

4. to place near, put to, serve, put on the table. [APPONO]
10. an oak grove, and oak forest. [QUERCETUM]
12. improvident, negligent [IMPROVIDUS]
14. discuss, debate, confer; betake oneself, devote. [CONFERO]
15. chain, fetters. [CATENA]
16. by much, by far, by a great deal, by a lot. [MULTO]
17. the elbow; a cubit. [CUBITUM]

Down

1. just as, according to. [PROUT]
2. to make fit, adapt, please, oblige, serve. [COMMODO]
3. growth, enlargement, increase. [AUCTUS]
5. offspring, descendants, posterity.. [PROLES]
6. the aristocratic party. [OPTIMATES]
7. to stretch, strain, try to prove. [INTENDO]
8. manfully. [VIRILITER]
9. wildly, savagely, fiercely, cruelly, roughly [TRUCULENTER]
10. square, a square. [QUADRATUS]
11. to serve, wait upon, provide, supply. [MINISTRO]
13. to call into question. [VOCO]
14. blind, sightless. [CAECUS]

Latin - 49

Across

6. bench, stool. [SCAMNUM]
7. twice. [BIS]
10. to bewail, weep for. [DEFLEO]
13. explanation, exposition. [EXPLICATUS]
15. to hurl, throw; put together, conjecture. [CONICIO]
16. to weigh, value, consider, judge, esteem. [PENDO]
18. painter [PICTOR]
21. accusation, calumny, charge. [CIMINATIO]
23. adv. far and wide, everywhere, scattered about. [PASSIM]
24. woman. [MULIER]
25. to make anew, refresh, revive, change, alter, invent. [NOVO]

Down

1. cat. [CATTUS]
2. flame, fire. [FLAMMA]
3. money. [PECUNIA]
4. gradually, little by little. [PAULATIM]
5. hire, employ for wages, among many other meanings. [CONDUCO]
8. to put to shame, disgrace. [INFAMO]
9. milky, of milk, milk-white. [LACTEUS]
11. enticement, allurement. [LENOCINIUM]
12. discuss. [DISPUTO]
14. filth, meanness, stinginess. [SORDES]
17. hold off, hold back, detain. [DETINEO]
19. sacred precinct, temple, sometimes church. [TEMPLUM]
20. ease, leisure, inactivity. [OTIUM]
22. road, route, journey. [ITER]

Latin - 50

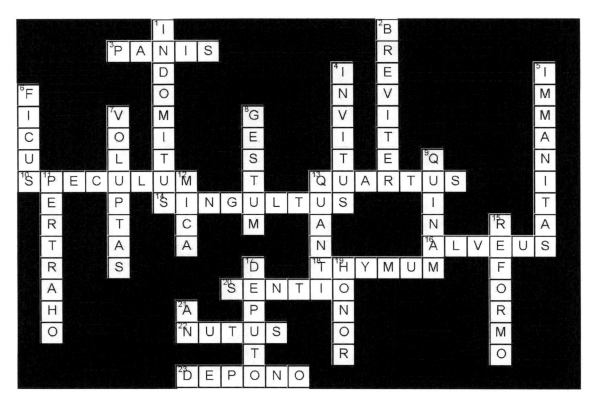

Across

3. bread. [PANIS]
10. mirror. [SPECULUM]
13. fourth. [QUARTUS]
14. sobbing, death rattle. [SINGULTUS]
16. hollow, basket, bed. [ALVEUS]
18. the herb thyme. [THYMUM]
20. feel, perceive, experience, hold an opinion, [SENTIO]
22. a nodding, nod, command, will. [NUTUS]
23. to put down, lay aside. [DEPONO]

Down

1. untamed, wild. [INDOMITUS]
2. briefly. [BREVITER]
4. unwilling, against one's will. [INVITUS]
5. savagery, frightfulness. [IMMANITAS]
6. fig tree. [FICUS]
7. pleasure. [VOLUPTAS]
8. carrying about, conduct . [GESTUM]
9. which? what? [QUINAM]
11. to drag, forcibly conduct, entice, allure. [PERTRAHO]
12. crumb, morsel, grain. [MICA]
13. for how much, at what price. [QUANTI]
15. to form again, mould anew. [REFORMO]
17. to count, estimate; prune, cut off. [DEPUTO]
19. honor, esteem, public office. [HONOR]
21. or [AN]

The Author

Michael Stachiw, Jr.

Michael is an Eagle Scout with hundreds of nights of camping and a Philmont trek under his belt. When he is not camping or participating in some other outdoor activity, he can be found studying law at New York University.

Made in the USA
Columbia, SC
09 December 2017